W9-BAO-770

To friends newly acquired and of long standing. It is with deep gratitude that we think of the fine people who shared their treasures with us and our readers. We humbly thank each of you for your friendship and hospitality.

# COUNTRY
# Furniture
## *and*
# Accessories
## *with prices*

Robert W. and Harriett Swedberg

Other books by Robert W. and Harriett Swedberg

*Off Your Rocker*
*Victorian Furniture Styles and Prices, Revised*
*Victorian Furniture Styles and Prices, Book II*
*Country Pine Furniture Styles and Prices*
*American Oak Furniture Styles and Prices*
*Wicker Furniture Styles and Prices*

Cover photograph by Perry L. Struse, Jr.
Location and country furniture
furnished by the
A B C Antique Shoppe
120 - 5th Street
West Des Moines, Iowa

All other photography by the authors
Printing and enlarging by Tom Luse

Library of Congress
Catalog Card Number 76-58066
ISBN 0-87069-411-1


10 9 8 7 6 5 4 3 2 1

Published by

Wallace-Homestead Book Company
1912 Grand Avenue
Des Moines, Iowa 50305

# Acknowledgments

The authors are especially grateful to the following collectors, dealers, and friends who unselfishly gave of their time and knowledge that this book might be compiled. We sincerely thank those who provided food and lodging after a long, work filled day. It gives us a warm feeling to be able to add more names to our growing list of newly made friends.

**Antique Forum**
Brookfield, Illinois

**The Antique Scene**
Rachel Cottrell
Moline, Illinois

**The Antique Scout**
Sharon and Richard Kreis
Hebron, Indiana

**The Antique Shop**
Fred, Doris, Bryan
Shawn, Damon, Darin Miller
Naponee, Indiana

**Antiques et cetera**
Dale and Jennie Rylander
Altoona, Illinois

**Antiques from the Valley**
Henry and Ruth Wargolet
Ontario, Wisconsin

**Bargain Bin**
Madge and Mary Foulk
Moline, Illinois

**Mr. and Mrs. Don C. Baum**

**Bittersweet Shop**
Mark and Gail Estabrooks
Gaylordsville, Connecticut

**Buttermilk Hill Antiques**
Terry Husk
Franklin, Pennsylvania

**Churchmouse**
Marilyn Johnson
Port Byron, Illinois

**Comus Antiques**
Tish and Bill Armstrong
New Market, Maryland

**Country Antiques**
Helen and Lester Lefstein
Quincy, Illinois

**Country Collectibles**
Mrs. Joan W. McCall
Kent, Connecticut

**Cubbyhole Antiques**
Bev Froelinger
Erie, Illinois

**Mary Davin's Antiques**
Iowa City, Iowa

**Delagrange Antiques**
George and Susan Delagrange
Jersomesville, Ohio

**The Dim Lantern Antiques**
Arlene Harrington
Franklin, Pennsylvania

**Edie's Emporium Antiques**
Reproductions & Gifts
Berkley Springs, West Virginia

**Farm House Antiques**
David and Edna Brown
Alexis, Illinois

**Garland's Antiques**
Garland Miller
Rocky's Antique Mall
Weyers Cave, Virginia

**Ralph and Virginia Gause**

**Arline Granger**
North Canton, Ohio

**Greenwood General Store**
Sharon Lord, dealer
Mary Little, proprietor
Greenwood, Illinois

**Dr. and Mrs. Carl Hamilton**

**Patricia Hayes Antiques**
Bittersweet Shop
Gaylordsville, Connecticut

**Hearth Antiques**
Susanne Edgerly
Bittersweet Shop
Gaylordsville, Connecticut

**Hickory Hill Antiques**
Pam Quanstrom
Galesburg, Illinois

**Holmes Antiques**
Cornwall Bridge, Connecticut

**The House and Barn**
Robert E. and Edna M. Miller
Webb's Mall #2
Centerville, Indiana

**Housman's Antiques**
Jan and Dick Housman
Pleasant Valley, Iowa

**Mike and Cheryl Jamison**

**Julianne and Jack Keim**

**Laub's Loft**
Marge and Myron Laub
Neponset, Illinois

**Lionwood Antiques**
Charles W. Hilliard
Bath, Ohio

**Kitty and Carl Marshall**

**Alberta and Dick Medd**

**Bill and Ruth Mehuys**

**Morticia's Abode**
Crete, Illinois

**Nana's Front Room Antiques**
Kathleen Constable
New Market, Maryland

**Richard Nelson**

**Plain and Fancy Antiques**
Franklin, Pennsylvania

**Michael, Marilyn,**
Jamey, and Alex Payne

**Pick's Antiques**
Allen Edwards and Loren Randle
Sparland, Illinois

**Red Apples Antiques**
Don and Alice Strube
Milwaukee, Wisconsin

**The Red Door**
Paul and Nancy Gorzelanski
Millard, Nebraska

**Red Pump Antiques**
Pat Carson, Fay Gustafson
Gerlaw, Illinois

**Clark, Carolyn**
Hilary, and Gavin Reed

**Robbie's Antiques**
Lewisburg, Ohio

**Rocky's Antique Mall**
Larry Carrier, Bruce Rosenwasser, Charles Lohr
Weyer's Cave, Virginia

**Room 102**
Marjorie Johnson and Barbara Krause
Richmond, Illinois

**Ricklef's Antiques**
Eloise and Doug
Anamosa, Iowa

**Earl Slack Antiques**
Earl J. Slack
Bittersweet Shop
Gaylordsville, Connecticut

**Small Stuff Antiques**
Lesley and Capt. Ken Denzin
Metairie, Louisiana

**Norval and Nedra Smith**

**Spinning Wheel Antiques**
Hazel Hanawalt
Woodland Park, Colorado

**Stitch Niche**
Carol Brewer and Nancy Cornish
Rock Island, Illinois

**The Strawberry Patch**
Sharon Parein
Cordova, Illinois

**Super Natural Antiques**
Jim and Carole Swenson
Janesville, Wisconsin

**Bill Van Dell**

**The Village Shop**
Susan Braucher
North Canton, Ohio

**Terry, Karen,**
Cody and Adam Watson

**Bill, Vivian,**
and Rhonda Yemm

# Contents

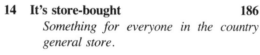

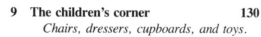

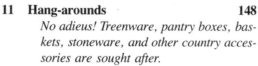

# Preface:
# How prices were obtained

**W**ebster's dictionary indicates that a guide shows the way, conducts, or leads. That's what this price guide attempts to do. It merely points the way to help you attach a value to objects you own or are seeking.

It is the result of extensive travel and consultation with dealers in at least one-third of the United States. The locales where the photographs were taken are listed. In all cases, the prices given are the ones assigned to the items by the dealers offering them for sale.

# 1  Sophisticated?

**H**ere's a paradoxical statement: "People in our section of the country are getting more sophisticated. They're beginning to buy country furniture." An antique dealer back East remarked, "A few years ago, nobody wanted it."

It's hard to associate the simple, functional lines of country with sophistication. Yet, the delicacy of uncluttered Shaker styling or the grace of a Windsor chair has a common country air with a dignified flare. Perhaps, the dealer is correct. Homeowners *are* becoming more sophisticated when they select country furniture.

There are those who disagree. A couple recently replaced their Victorian furniture with country and primitive. A visitor wailed, "Oh, what did you do with all your beautiful walnut furniture?" Another person sort of sniffed and remarked, "Well, it's . . ." Then, paused to search for an inoffensive word . . . "Interesting." The response of another friend was hearty. "This is more like it! Country's warm, and this is an expression of you."

This book is for those who find country compatible with their life styles. Because wares of the 1700s are mainly museum quality, they will be ignored. Furniture and accessories of the 1800s and early 1900s will be included because they are available and within the price range of the general public.

A country setting with woodbox, 38″ wide, 16″ deep, 31″ high. In Illinois, **$125;** wagon with wooden wheels, metal rim, **$175;** hay fork and miscellaneous accessory items.

## Country

Country pieces have fewer frills than the works of urban artisans. Frequently, Ma wanted an article for a specific place or purpose. If Pa had manual dexterity and the proper tools, he completed his task easily. Or, he "made do" using bits of wood (any kind or mixture) and a few rough tools. Frequently, this man could not fashion joints or add frills so he kept the lines and construction simple. Sometimes a country cabinetmaker completed the job.

Painted fancy chairs with bright stencils have been made in factories from the 1820s until the present. They are often called Hitchcock chairs. In Connecticut, **$90.**

A maul, a heavy mallet for pounding, was a tool most frontiersmen owned because they could make their own. This maul with a 5½″ diameter, 4″ high burled base is not a common variety. In Nebraska, **$38.**

And, that's what country is — functional furniture and accessories designed to meet a definite need.

Early examples were made by hand. Then, as the 1700s departed, the Industrial Revolution came. It offered factory production of machined and standardized component parts that were interchangeable.

In 1798, Eli Whitney sought to supply the United States government with muskets in which the barrels were identical. One man at a machine made batches of barrels. Another worker made all the triggers. Each man contributed a specific part rather than creating a whole gun. Assemblers then put the musket pieces together.

This represented mass production and the start of the assembly line concept. Manufacturers of chairs followed suit, as did Eli Terry with clocks, for example. By the 1870s, water and steam were providing the power to operate machines in factories.

However, through the years Ma has continued to ask Pa to make something for their home.

A middle-aged woman recently exhibited rough chairs that were made to order in the 1940s for her rural Missouri mother by a hill man, who quickly fashioned the wooden parts with his penknife. Weaving of the rush seats waited several years until he could gather the proper reeds in the wild grasses of the shoreline bogs flooded by the Sherman River. Those chairs aren't very old — but they are country furniture. If you were not aware of their origin, the uneven, unmatched hand work and the use of swamp rush, as opposed to modern twisted paper rush, might make the chairs appear older.

Most rustics knew a little bit about a lot of things, dabbled in various trades, and were almost self-sufficient. Like the Missouri man who made the rush bottom chairs, each had a knife for cutting, carving, and protection. What additional tools did pioneers own to construct their homes and furnishings? An ax chopped down trees. A maul (heavy mallet) was a pounder, and froes (or frows) sliced shingles. An adz (adze) was an axlike tool for wood shaving. It had a crosswise blade.

Few pioneers possessed such fancy tools as a scribe to incise guidelines on wood, gouges and chisels to cut and shape, a square to measure angles, calipers to indicate thickness so matching parts such as legs would be nearly the same, leveling and smoothing planes, and gimlets for boring. It was the rare family that had a foot-treadle lathe on which to make turnings. Thus, legs and rungs were usually plain.

# Primitives

Country and primitives are cousins. Primitives are considered cruder. They were made to meet a need for furniture, but the maker lacked skill or put them together hurriedly to suit the purpose. Primitives also include farm items, nostalgic survivors from small town stores, or occupational items.

Today obsolete articles from mail order houses attract buyers because great grandma had them. The list is long. It includes factory produced washday and ironing needs such as boilers, tubs, wringers, trivets, and sadirons. Many old wood burning stoves serve as end tables or again provide heat now that saving energy is stressed. Water pumps and chamber sets recall the days before plumbing. Butter churns and woodboxes also have been rescued from oblivion. Whether these are genuine antiques or collectible articles of a more recent date, they accomplish two purposes. Such articles provide a link with the past and lend a charm all their own when invited into modern homes.

The vocabulary of antiquing includes words such as marriage, cobbled, reproduction, and fake. Let's take a run-through.

Wooden grease pot, 7″ by 5″ at the top, 12″ high, for a Conestoga wagon is a hand carved primitive. The egg beside it indicates its size. In Illinois, **$125.**

The M. Brown Co. of Wapakoneta, Ohio, made this 4-gallon bentwood butter churn in the early 1900s. In Illinois, **$215.**

A walnut bookcase top from a secretary desk has been united with a light country table to form a marriage. Top, 39″ wide, 11½″ deep, 54″ high; table base, 40½″ wide, 27½″ deep, 26″ high. In Illinois, **$450.**

This is a cobbled wainscot cupboard base that someone apparently tried to convert into a dry sink by inserting a well. 37″ wide, 15″ deep, 35″ high. In Illinois, **$75.**

# Marriage?

There's no romance in a marriage of antiques. Greed generally joins two unrelated pieces together to appear as an original piece of furniture in the hope that it will attract a buyer. It is a questionable practice. Such a marriage to deceive is frowned upon.

Occasionally, a dealer does not promote such a union. At an antiques show, two pine pieces stood near each other in a booth. A customer examined both. Then she asked the dealer, "Please set this small cupboard with the glass doors on top of that double commode. I'd like to see how they go together."

Since the lines of the two pieces were compatible, the resulting unit was attractive. "I'll take them," the matchmaker said. "I can use each separately or I can combine them as one."

One common practice is to add a glass enclosed bookcase to the top of a drop lid desk to form a secretary. Sometimes the base is a soft maple table with a drawer. It has been stained dark to resemble walnut. The bookcase part actually is walnut. Small nailholes around the top indicate some changes have been made. Perhaps, a cornice was removed to give the shelves a simple country look for a better match with the table's style. The proportions are not correct. The table is too low. An antique frequently will have space cut out at the rear of the table desk — probably to save precious wood. There is no recessed section, and it's obvious that this was always just a table.

# Cobbled?

If furniture has had major alterations, it is called cobbled. Perhaps, the ceiling in a modern home is not high enough to accommodate tall furniture. The owners will slice off part of the furniture to make it fit. The high, high headboard on late Victorian beds might have undergone such surgery — the mid-section removed and the ornate top reattached to the stub.

At times, a "colonial bed" emerged when a dealer stripped the paint from a cottage bed of the 1890s in order to reveal the pine or poplar beneath. The next step was to gentle the bed's lines and convert it to an older style. After the bed was lowered, the price zoomed.

Occasionally, open pewter cupboards began life as closed cupboards. For a novice, such switches are difficult to detect because old wood is used. Be aware of styles. Check to see if stain has been used to blend freshly exposed clean surfaces with neighboring parts that have patina, the natural darkening with age caused by exposure to air, dust, and light.

Certain repairs required to restore an article are acceptable. Who wants an unstable table in need of glue to steady it or a chair that begs for re-rushing so it has a firm seat? Worn drawer slides on a centenarian case piece should be repaired if they are to function smoothly.

A woman was delighted to acquire the small chair her husband's mother had rocked in as a child. One arm was missing, and her son cautioned, "Don't replace it. You'll ruin the chair's antique value." However, the rocker wasn't useful or attractive as is was. A skillful restoration was certainly called for.

Be cautious about buying furniture that needs repairs. Professional restoration may not be worth the expense unless the furniture is a sought-after piece or pre-dates 1800. It is difficult to discover something of that vintage, and the price is usually too high for the ordinary family budget. These factors tend to make such furniture worthy of restoration. Furniture by famous cabinetmakers also deserves repair. As a general rule, it is wiser to invest a little more money and acquire a good example rather than to end up with a mediocre piece after extensive restoration.

The broken original rockers were replaced with new ones to make this rocker serviceable again. 38″ high. In Connecticut, **$85.**

A handcrafted hanging shelf of recent origin made of old pine. 26″ wide, 6½″ deep, 27″ high. In Illinois, **$65.**

Reproduction Pennsylvania dry sink was marked NEW on its price tag. 29″ wide, 15½″ deep, 33½″ high. In Pennsylvania, **$155.**

Hanging case with an ogee front has not been stripped of its mahogany veneer to expose the pine wood underneath. 17½″ wide, 5″ deep, 25½″ high. In Illinois, **$155.**

# Reproduction? Fake?

Windsor chairs hit the American scene in the early 1700s, and they have been made with variations ever since. When a product serves the public well, it can enjoy a lengthy life. Unless a Windsor of current times is sold for old, it is not fraudulent merchandise. The term fake implies any misrepresentation. It is considered deceitful to lie about the age, style, and history of furniture, or to falsely attribute a piece to a recognized craftsman. Sale of a reproduction is not misleading if a purchaser is told that it is new. Only when a buyer is encouraged to believe that he is acquiring an antique does the transaction become spurious.

Here's another practice that should sound an alert. To veneer means to cover a base wood with a thin sheet of a more decorative grain. At times, people who prefer the country look steam or soak off this covering on frames, chests, or clocks to bare the original pine or poplar beneath. This also is done if the veneer is in bad shape. An example is a frame with a double S curve. It's an ogee frame that dates prior to 1840. Mahogany veneer covers its surface. When this frame is given the steam or bath treatment, the double curve remains to tattle: "I may be plain as can be, but see my S, I'm still an ogee." Think ogee when you see such frames.

Now, you are ready to inspect furniture inside and out — and a flashlight helps. Tips on the following pages will assist you to answer the question: What is old?

# How Old?

It's difficult to determine the age of country pieces because people like to work with their hands and have done so in every generation. One man goes to flea markets, garage sales, and antique shows to shop for old woodworking tools. He chooses those he can use to make pseudo-antiques for his home. Sometimes, other capable women and men are strapped for cash and they build their own. Most of these people do not adhere to old assembly methods or use tools of the past. This makes it possible to distinguish their objects from those of yore. Formal furniture follows fashions and can be pinpointed to certain years. Country, built from need, cannot be restricted to a period of time. It is incorrect to think that all desks or tables from the 1800s were made by hand. Inexpensive cottage-type products machined in factories have been available for more than one hundred and fifty years. Sometimes, hand touches such as applied carvings, painting, or stenciling were added at the factory.

Country furniture has other confusing facets. At times, a rural cabinetmaker went to the nearby big city and was impressed when he saw the popular styles of the day. When he returned home, he tried to duplicate them. Because of this, there are country pieces that follow the lines popularized by English furniture designers Chippendale, Hepplewhite, and Sheraton. The works of these craftsmen were duplicated in America some years after their debut in Great Britain. Thomas Chippendale's influence was felt in this country from about the late 1750s through 1790, but the ideas of George Hepplewhite and Thomas Sheraton were still in vogue in the early 1800s. Naturally, styles would seep into backwoods locales at a much later date — after settlements were well established. Only then could frontiersmen turn from the fight for survival and give their attention to other aspects of life.

Note the gently tapering legs that follow the Hepplewhite style on this pine country stand. 30½″ wide, 23½″ deep, 30″ high. In Iowa, **$285.**

# Joiner's joints

A joint refers to the way two pieces of wood are joined together in constructing furniture. The skilled craftsman who mastered this art was called a joiner. Here are some terms of his trade:

**Scribe line** — The mark left by a pointed instrument is called a scribe. It cuts a shallow, narrow groove to indicate where and how two parts of a piece of furniture should be joined together.

**Mortise and tenon** — A tongue or thick prong that sticks out on a piece of wood is called a tenon. The mortise is a corresponding hole or slot in another piece of wood into which the tenon fits snugly. The joint is of green wood and the

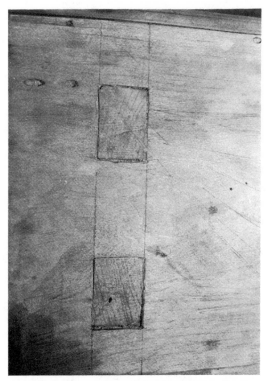

A mortise and tenon joint. Notice the distinct scribe lines made by the cabinetmaker to mark the width of the tenon on the top of an Ohio Amish footstool.

A wedge has been driven into the top of a leg to force it to expand and fit tightly. The three other legs on this narrow slaughtering bench are also wedged.

The shelf compartments in a hanging wall cabinet are tongue and grooved.

tenon has been seasoned (dried). The hole shrinks as it dries and grips the already shrunken tongue more securely. A wooden pin driven through both boards at the point of contact assures a permanent union. Mortise and tenon were joints used in all periods of American furniture. The slats on a chair back enter the uprights in this way. Head- and footboards for beds commonly have prongs that fit into slots in the posts. Aprons on tables and case pieces may be joined this way.

**Wedge**    A piece of wood that tapers to a thin edge is known as a wedge. Sometimes, a wedge was forced into its hole or slot. When a tenon can be seen, it is referred to as "open" and can receive the wedge expansion treatment. For example: When the legs on a bench extended to the top of the seat, a wedge was often hammered in to cause the end of the leg to expand and assure a tight fit.

**Tongue and groove**    When a continuous tongue protrudes at the end of a wooden piece and is inserted into a corresponding groove in another board with which it is to be united, it is called a tongue and groove joint. Shelf compartments could be joined by a tongue and groove. Wainscoted dry sinks also used this contruction.

A wainscot dry sink has a tongue and groove construction. 50″ wide, 21″ deep, 34½″ high. In Wisconsin, **$545.**

**Miter joint**     When two boards are cut at a slant so that they form a right angle when fitted together, the result is called a miter joint. Pegs or nails driven through both boards secure them. Glue is an added aid. Square and rectangular frames are joined in this way.

This ill-fitting miter joint was found on a pine picture frame that was originally mahogany veneered.

Two drawers are examples of lap or rabbet joint construction.

This drawer section and the end view of a knife box show butt construction.

**Lap or rabbet joint**

When a right-angle cut in the front of one board fits smoothly in a right-angle cut in the back of another, a rabbet or lap joint is formed. At times, a right-angle cut at the end of one board is placed to overlap the edge of another straight board. Similar notches are used on the backs of case pieces. Such joints often are found in drawers.

**Butt joint**

Two straight pieces of wood are butted against each other and fastened when a butt joint is used. Early joiners pegged them in position. Later, nails and glue were used. A six-board chest is a wooden box with a lift lid. It receives its name because six whole boards were used to build it. Their edges were usually butted together. Drawers can be butted together.

**Dovetail joint**

Triangular projections on one piece of wood fit with precision into a matching cut in another board. These have a remote resemblance to a dove's tail; hence, the name. They interlock in jigsaw puzzle fashion. Some skilled craftsmen used dainty dovetails and more of them, while larger dovetails were the product of cruder workmanship. Incised lines made by the worker's sharp, pointed scribe showed the outline and spacing desired. A straight line at the end indicated the depth required. Machines do not need similar assistance. Dovetails are frequently seen on trunks or boxes and on drawers where the sides meet the fronts.

Dovetail construction, with the observable scribe lines, joins the four boards on this dowry chest. 37" wide, 20" deep, 20" high. In Wisconsin, **$235.**

America's rich forests supplied woods of all varieties from dark to light and hard to soft. They included oak, hickory, ash, chestnut, elm, beech, fruitwoods (including cherry), butternut, walnut, cedar, sycamore, gum, pine, maple, and poplar. Many people think of light-colored woods such as pine, poplar, and maple when they mention country or primitive furniture, but the other species also were used. It's the simplicity of lines and the details of construction that classify the pieces.

How can these construction techniques help you determine the age of a piece of furniture? *Examine a drawer.* It has much to tell:

*Look for scribe lines.* These incised lines indicate hand workmanship. The cabinetworker scratched them into the wood to serve as construction guides. Where should two pieces meet? How should they be lined up? How deep and how big should the joint be? Scribe lines provide the answers. Machines don't need such help.

A drawer bottom from an early nineteenth century butternut jelly cupboard shows the inundations left by the cabinetmaker's plane. The rough, beveled edges allow the bottom to fit into the sides and front, where channels had been cut.

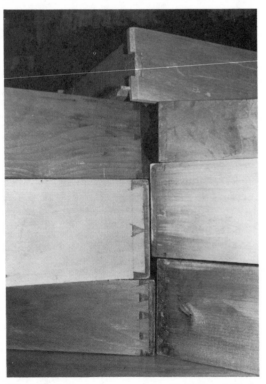

This stack of drawers shows examples of handmade dovetailing and their scribe lines. Machine-made dovetailing with a scalloped edge and perfectly round dowels can be seen on the bottom right drawer.

*Look at tool marks.* The bottom of this pre-1840 drawer was hand planed. The inundations left on the wood can be seen as well as felt. The edges were bevelled on the front and two sides in order to fit the grooves in the outer structure of the drawer. The edges are irregular.

*Note the dovetails,* the triangular projections in one piece of wood that fit with precision into a matching cut in another board to interlock in jigsaw puzzle fashion. A clue to the dovetails made by hand? Watch for uneven spacing and slight deviations in size and shape. Examples of dovetailing with machine-made scallops and perfectly round pegs have been found in antiques of the late 1800s. Early pegs are not perfectly round, but have a slightly squared-off appearance.

*Look for a butt joint* where two pieces are united and secured with pegs or nails. A vintage drawer may have a rabbet or lap joint with right angles cut into adjacent boards. Examples are shown under joiner's joints.

# Refractory paints

Refractory paints are stubborn and tend to resist removers. Their stick-to-itiveness gave them this name. Purists shout, "Preserve that paint!" They seek to save history and heritage from going down the drain.

Researchers state that the colors of the 1600s were red, black, yellow, and green. As the 1700s ended, milk paints in reds, blues, and grays emerged. People mixed their own, and they discovered that milk made a good, lasting base. Casein, a protein that is one of the main constituents of milk, is also used to make glue. No wonder that milk paint has stuck around for generations!

It is this old paint that should be retained, not the coats applied at a later date. A woman remarked that as a child she painted her ancestral bed whenever her room colors were changed. She painted the bed purple and white. She globbed on pink. She tried ivory. As an adult, she stripped these multiple applications down to the original wood and was disgusted with her past paint jobs. This type of repainting should be removed. It is the original that is desirable.

People who restore antiques say it is possible to strip coats of paint by gently and carefully applying a remover and taking off one layer at a time. It takes hours, but they feel the results justify their efforts. They are seeking to preserve a part of the past. For this purpose, a paste-type remover is easier to control than a water-rinse product.

It is said that pioneers threw in leftovers to concoct batches of paint. Excess eggs or coffee grounds joined milk. Colors were obtained from berries, plants, clay, or the blood of butchered animals. Indigo for blue hues was an expensive import from India until Georgia and South Carolina grew these plants, which are members of the pea family. After 1897, this natural plant dye was replaced by a synthetic developed from aniline, a coal-tar product.

In the late 1700s and early 1800s, it was possible to buy manufactured materials that could

An open cupboard from upper New York State, circa 1840, retains its old red paint on the outside, but the green inside has been retouched slightly. 43″ wide, 13½″ deep, 72″ high. In Wisconsin, **$875.**

be mixed to make paint. It was not until 1867 that pre-mixed, ready-to-use paints were marketed. Of course, many people still stirred up their own.

Since the soft, faded paints of long ago connect the past with the present, it is good to retain them. If their worn surfaces don't please you, rejuvenate them. Strip them with a paint remover or scraper. But do retain a little of the old finish on an underneath portion to show age and indicate that the component parts are original.

Some people want furniture left unretouched because they feel changes diminish value. Others touch up battered surfaces. A modern formula for milk paint calls for powdered milk to be mixed with water to form a mixture the consistency of paint. Any color may be produced by adding dry pigments available from paint or art supply stores. Bright tones can be muted by adding black or brown pigments. Now, you have a modern milk-base (casein) refractory paint that is akin to glue.

23

The owner of this rocker painted melted kitchen wax over the design on the back rail and then painted the chair black. When the paint had dried, she gently scraped the wax from the design. 24½" arm to arm, 38" high. In Iowa, **$185.**

Here is an 1879 formula for milk paint found in *Ransom's Family Recipe Book,* 1879, Free to Everyone; published by D. Ransom, Son & Co., Buffalo, New York.

> Milk Paint — for barns, any color. Mix water lime* with skim milk to proper consistency to apply with brush, and it is ready to use. It will adhere well to wood — smooth or rough — to brick, mortar, or stone, where oil has not been used. The result will be as durable as the best oil paint. Any color may be had by using colors dissolved in whisky.

---

*Water lime is calcium hydroxide that usually can be purchased at a pharmacy. Shake the water lime in one gallon of distilled water on and off for about an hour before using it.

# Wormholes?

"Wormholes" do not help indicate the age of furniture. These small circles are made by the larvae of beetles. "Bugs" can enter wood at any time, and they may be chomping on your furniture, now if a thin dust is present. Seek immediate aid to eliminate them. The holes vary in size, from pinprick to tack or small nail-tip. The bugs prefer certain woods such as cherry. They dislike noisy vibrations so they avoid stairs. Infestation will be more pronounced in one area than another. Some people fake these larvae marks, thinking that an illusion of age is created. Because larvae meander on a zigzag path, a wire usually cannot be plunged straight into an authentic wormhole.

# Hardware?

Handles are called "hardware" although they may be made of metal, glass, wood, ceramics, or molded materials. Clues to age include escutcheons (keyhole outlines and backplates for bail handles), hinges, hasps, metal bands, locks, screws, and nails.

Furniture catalogs of the mid-1870s offered Victorian chests of drawers with or without handles. Mirrors were optional and called "toilets" because they aided a person in grooming. Hair combed? Face thoroughly washed? Tie straight?

**Handles**    Various types of handles were popular in 1837-1901 when Queen Victoria reigned in England. These included wooden knobs, round or mushroom in shape; carved or occasionally molded wooden fruits or acorns, and drop pulls referred to as teardrops. Simple furniture usually had wooden peg pulls, whittled pulls, flattened knobs, or pulls of white porcelain. Doors might have catches with wooden tongues that twisted to fit into grooves.

Handles just prior to and after 1900 might be cast metal rectangles

The porcelain knobs on this homemade cabinet are considered hardware, and each drawer is a cheese box with the original printing. In Illinois, **$65.**

Low, one-door base cabinet with wooden knob and clasp. 38″ wide, 20″ deep, 38″ high. In Illinois, **$165.**

Storage piece has cast metal handles, with brass escutcheons on the bottom two drawers. 38″ wide, 11½″ deep, 23″ high. In Illinois, **$245.**

with openings at the bottom to offer a hand grip. These handles matched angular door catches. All bore identical designs because they were molded. Trunks and lift-lid chests generally had leather or iron handles. Infrequently, twisted rope or wooden handles were used. Today, an unused hole shows that the original handles on drawers were removed. Dirt and wax cause a slight buildup around pulls that have been attached for years. This encrustation can be seen readily. The outline of a removed handle shows because the surface beneath is lighter in color. This area was covered and protected from exposure to air, light, and dirt that darken wood. These signs speak for the handles and say, "Well, we've been switched."

**Hinges and locks**

The blacksmith was a respected, skilled workman who heated iron over a fire to make it malleable so that he could place it on his anvil and pound it into desired shapes. His products were hammered out, and none precisely matched. These irregularities indicate hand work. Such iron hinges and handles had names suggested by their shapes. Can't you visualize rat tail, butterfly, or H-hinges? Hasp locks and cotter pins were products of the blacksmith shop. A cotter pin is a fastener that has a loop head and two parallel prongs. It resembles a bobby pin or a hairpin. After a cotter pin is inserted, it is held in place by separating and spreading the two prong ends. Such objects that were pounded into shape are referred to as hand-wrought. Cast metal products generally were formed all alike in a mold. Occasionally, metal handles or locks will have a patent date. This tells you the object was made sometime in or after that year because patents protect inventions for seventeen years.

**Escut-cheons**  These keyhole outlines may be of brass, iron, wood, bone, or ivory, and various kinds are associated with different periods. Plain ones would be inset. Those with ornate designs would be attached to the outside. Escutcheons are less apt to be changed than handles that are worn from constant tugging and pulling.

The ends of two cotter pins secure the bail handle on the top side of this small trunk. Their spread ends are irregular, which indicates they were hand wrought.

Brass escutcheon is evident on this trunk that has retained most of its original red paint. 29″ wide, 17″ deep, 22″ high. In Illinois, **$275.**

The five smallest nails in this grouping taper to a point on all four sides. After 1800, cut nails tapered on the two opposite sides and were almost as thick at the bottom as near the top. The largest nails visible seem to fit this description. Old nails secure these wooden dividing devices on the work area of a circa 1840 cobbler's bench.

**Nails**   Nails have long been known to man. In 1786, Ezekiel Reed of Massachusetts invented a machine to make nails, but they were generally hand forged until about 1800. Hand-wrought nails taper to a point on all four sides and are of a fine quality iron that endures. After 1800, cut nails were made by machine. These taper on two opposite sides to a bluntish point and have square heads. They do not have the strength of their predecessors. It was not until the late 1860s that a machine was perfected to make round headed and circular shanked steel nails. In the 1890s, the modern wire nail with its round head and body and pointed tip was developed. Since it is currently possible to purchase square-headed nails, their presence in not a conclusive sign of age.

Nails usually were imperfectly spaced and not countersunk into the wood when hammered into place. With age, wood frequently appears to swell over the exposed heads slightly, and a dark ring forms around them.

**Screws**   Early blunt-end screws of iron or brass probably were first used around 1690. Their heads were flat, not perfect circles; grooves were irregular as were the spirals. In the 1700s, the brass (an alloy of copper, zinc, and perhaps tin) used for screws was a yellowish-white, probably because it had less copper content. Machine-made screws from about 1800 still had flat tips, but were more uniform and had sharper edges. By the mid-1800s, modern pointed screws with symmetrical threads were available. Deeper screwdriver slots were properly positioned in the middle of the round heads. They were even, not crooked or off-center as older examples.

# Pegs?

Furniture makers have used pegs since the trade began. Pegs are not difficult to make and are less expensive than metal screws or nails. Hand-made pins (pegs) are not perfectly round. They may even appear slightly square in shape. Often, pegs protrude, probably because the wood around them dried and shrank with time. Occasionally, pegs are inserted in odd places in an attempt to make customers think that a piece is old. Pegs reinforce a mortise and tenon joint on a door, or they may help hold a drawer together. Remember, pegs were used for functional purposes. Perfectly round pins appeared in the late 1800s and early 1900s. They were machine made.

Irregular, almost square pegs, can be seen on the baseboard of a small, early nineteenth century trunk.

This long-legged chair was probably pulled up to a tall desk where its occupant sat for hours daily. The rung where the worker placed his feet is almost worn through. 48″ high. In Connecticut, **$150.**

# Signs of Wear?

Long ago, men often relaxed by tilting their chairs against the wall. This gradually smoothed off the chair's back legs at the rear. Finials also became worn from constant wall contact. Children whose feet didn't reach to the floor placed them on the front rung of their chairs, and a scooped rung resulted. Wood became worn wherever hands continually touched, such as around drawer pulls or on the arms of chairs. A broom constantly hitting the base of furniture left mars. A dustrag in time dulled edges and sharp features. Constant scrubbing of kitchen or dining room tables showed. Painted or artificially grained chairs mellowed and developed slight imperfections as human bodies wiggled and rubbed off parts of stenciled fruits and flowers. Lids on trunks were constantly opened and banged shut. Drawers suffered the same, and their bottom edges wore away unevenly from continual abrasive sliding across the runners. The middle drawer usually showed the greatest wear. Look for such signs of wear — and suspect any that are in doubtful locations.

The worn paint and sagging cane seat attest to the heavy use this rocker has seen. 43″ high. In Connecticut, **$275.**

# Glass?

Glass also offers age tips. Very early cupboards tended to be the open type without doors. If glass panes were used, they would be small and separated by wooden dividers. Glass from the 1700s and before was hand blown (by human lung power) and the hot glob of metal (term for molten glass) left a bump in the center of the pane, which many call a bull's eye. Impurities in the silica (sand) used in the formula produced a greenish cast in the glass. Such imperfections can be seen and felt. These old panes are a rarity. Glass panes made during a large part of the 1800s have a wavy appearance, and this distorted look is treasured. Usually not all the original panes in a vintage cupboard would remain unbroken. It was not until the latter part of the nineteenth century that a technique was developed to make large sizes of flat sheet glass.

Corner cupboard in cherry has twelve panes of old, wavy glass. 45″ wide, 17½″ deep, 82″ high. In Iowa, **$1,350.**

# Patina? Shrinkage?

Some authorities do not stress patina as an indicator of age. Others feel that wood shrinkage is not reliable. Both views will be discussed.

Patina should be evenly distributed on exposed surfaces. The insides of case pieces would not be as dark as the outsides, but should have mellowed slightly. The bottom of the lowest drawer in a desk or chest is exposed more than the bottom of the top one and should have the deeper color tone that comes with age.

Most authorities feel wood shrinks across the grain with age, causing gaps to appear on table tops or in the butted backs of case pieces. The top of a round table measures slightly smaller across the grain than going with it. An internationally recognized expert with the United States Department of Agriculture Forest Products Laboratory does not consider shrinkage a reliable age indicator. He says a crack appears in a wooden bowl when the weather is dry and the wood contracts. High humidity can cause the pieces to swell and meet again. This can happen on the split sides of a washstand.

# Wood?

Frequently, wood about an inch thick was used in the construction of furniture dating to the 1800s. An entire top could be made from one piece of wood or perhaps with two pieces of random widths. Early legs usually were turned from one piece. Today, some turnings are made from layers of wood glued together. Walnut was the predominate furniture wood from about 1840 until oak started to take over in the late 1800s. Necessity and the demands of style brought about this change. The walnut forests were becoming depleted because of wasteful forestry practices. Conservation became a political theme. The cost of wood rose, and the tops of tables and chests soon were made of lumber cut in standard sizes and joined together. Random widths and thick woods were on their way out.

# Tools?

Tools of the past leave marks to attest that a piece of furniture was not made recently.

**Scribe**    Using a scribe, a farmer-craftsman incised lines to serve as guides. In making a chair, he used the lines to indicate where the slats fit into the posts or the rungs in the legs. The marks helped him put the pieces together.

**Lathe**    Operated by hand, a lathe rotated slowly as it held a piece of wood against a cutting tool to shape an object such as a table leg. Narrow gouges appeared in the finished work as a result of the slow turning. The lathe operator frequently judged the accuracy of his design by eyeballing his work, which is why each resulting leg differed slightly.

**Calipers**    Thickness and diameter are measured by calipers, and further prove that no legs were created equal. Craftsmen did use calipers to help keep sizes fairly uniform.

**Saws**    The pattern left by cuttings from a saw are called kerf marks. Before 1850, a straight blade bit into the wood, and left up-and-down parallel rows. The circular saw probably reached American shores by 1820 and spread to most locales by 1850. The trail it left on wood was circular or semicircular rows of lines. Suspect a bit of sleight-of-hand when both types of saw marks appear in one piece of furniture — unrelated pieces probably have been combined.

**Planes**    An early jack plane removed portions of wood or smoothed surfaces. It made waves across the grain, and these inundations can be seen and felt. Close one eye and sight along the edge of a molding (a continuous edging carved in or applied to wood). When made by a hand-operated plane, unevenness can be detected. A machine would follow a regular path. Applied molding was pegged in place or fastened with small nails. Country furniture ornamentation was plain.

So, as a first-grade reader might say, "Look, Jane, look. See the marks." The differences are clues to age. And if you take a whiff of the old wood, it has a smell all its own. With all this knowledge, you are prepared to *see, feel, and smell* the difference between objects from the past and those that are new. Be observant. Ask questions. Visit antique shops, and museums. You'll make some bad buys. Everyone does. That's part of the quest. Soon, you'll be so smart you'll brag about the bargains you have snared. It's up to you now. Go forth, but keep learning.

# 2   Windsor chairs

In a folk tale about Windsor chairs, a king named George III ruled a country called England. While hunting, he was inconvenienced by a sudden rain and sought refuge in a peasant cottage. Naturally, he appropriated the one guest chair. His corpulent frame found comfort in its roominess, so he immediately ordered copies for his home, Windsor Castle. Henceforth, chairs of this type were called Windsors in honor of the king's castle.

This circa 1790 Windsor is now at Mount Vernon. It retains its original brownish-yellow paint with black trim in the grooves. Note the splayed legs.

Nay, say the skeptics (and historians). The style predates this man's reign (1760-1820) by at least fifty years, and some trace it back much further. It is known that in 1730 a craftsman advertised Windsor chairs. In addition, a Windsor chair reached the English colonies in America in the early 1700s, years before King George III ascended the throne. These facts cause authoriites to believe that the chair was named for the market town of Windsor, near where the chair was made.

Across the Atlantic Ocean, who found Windsors comfortable? Many of the rebellious colonial leaders did. The chambers in Independence Hall in Philadelphia were furnished with Windsors. It is thought that benches of this style were used to accommodate male spectators. (A woman's place was in the home.)

Thomas Jefferson reportedly used a Windsor with a wide flat arm that served as a writing surface when he composed the first draft of the Declaration of Independence. Speculation is that he may have designed the chair himself because it differs from other writing Windsors. The arm on Jefferson's pivoted so it could be swung in closer to the user. Another variation was its revolving seat.

A 1785 painting, which commemorated the signing of the Declaration of Independence, depicts Benjamin Franklin in the center foreground seated in a bow-back Windsor.

When President George Washington's second term in office was ending, he was eager to retire to his Mount Vernon plantation. He purchased twenty-four "ovel back" (sic) chairs on May 16, 1796, from Gilbert and Robert Gaw of Philadelphia and soon after ordered three more. All twenty-seven cost forty-eight dollars. They were to be shipped down the Potomac River, and Washington wrote his plantation manager that they were to be placed in the "New Room."

After Washington's widow died, the contents of Mount Vernon were sold and became widely dispersed. No one knows what happened to George Washington's twenty-seven Gaw chairs. In 1970, five samples of marked Gaw Windsors were found in Moline, Illinois, by the Mount Vernon Ladies Association that maintains Washington's home. All five chairs had the burned-in brand mark of the maker, R. Gaw, on the underside of the seats. Two also had a tacked-on paper label attesting that the Windsors were made and sold by Robert Gaw of Philadelphia. Later in the year, when the owners agreed that all five chairs should go to Mount Vernon, they offered to ship them. This would not do. The home's administrative assistant, accompanied by a uniformed guard, personally packed and loaded the chairs. Purists, who believe original finishes should be retained, found the five chairs in a good state of preservation. These Windsors may never be traced to the Washingtons, although their buff paint does match the woodwork in Mount Vernon's "New Room."

The second president, John Adams, favored a Windsor with a high bow-back. His son, John Quincy Adams who became the sixth president in 1825, also liked that chair. Thus, four early presidents are known to have owned Windsors — Washington, John and John Quincy Adams, and Jefferson.

In May 1796 President George Washington purchased twenty-seven "ovel back chairs" from Gilbert and Robert Gaw of Philadelphia. This is the paper label found on the underside of one of the chair seats.

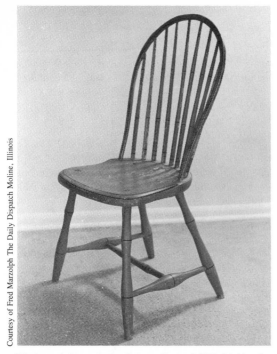

Windsor chair made by Robert Gaw of Philadelphia. In addition to the paper label shown, it bears the burned mark, "R. Gaw."

This English Windsor chair has a pierced splat in the middle of the back, 25″ arm to arm, 43″ high. In Illinois, **$395.**

How do the chairs made on opposite sides of the Atlantic compare? Quality English Windsor chairs have a more masculine appearance than their American counterparts. The most notable feature that differentiates the two is the design of the backs. English examples generally have a middle splat that is lacking in American styles. In addition, the English Windsor has a stouter appearance because its legs are socketed near the edge of the seat and do not slant out so much as the American version. Perhaps, this is why the Windsor originally was considered a country chair suitable for English cottages or lawns.

In Philadelphia, in about the mid-1820s, chair makers who started copying the English Windsor began revising its lines. (Later, chair makers in other sections of the country were to add distinctive touches of their own.) Instead of the central splat, they used tapering spindles. They chamfered (cut in at a slant) the bottom of the seats to reduce the bulky look and drilled holes for the legs at an angle about three inches in from the edge of the seat so the legs slanted out more. Many times, legs went completely through the seat and showed at the top, where a wedge and glue secured them. Some legs were fitted into holes drilled three-fourths of the way into the seat. The stretchers generally were recessed and H-shaped. While the American Windsor had a daintier, more graceful appearance than its British prototype, its thorough construction gave it strength.

In addition, two mutations were attributed to Yankee ingenuity. One was the writing Windsor. Additional spindles that were set in an extension of the seat supported a wide, flat arm. Sometimes, one or two drawers were added. One might be under the arm and another the seat. (Today, school desks are sometimes made with a writing arm and a drawer beneath the seat.)

These loop-back Windsors have splayed legs, H-stretchers and thick, shaped seats with the underside chamfered or bevelled to diminish the heavy look. **$2,500** for the set of six which don't precisely match. The mortise and tenoned harvest table has two drop leaves. 75″ long, 44″ wide with leaves up, 27½″ high. In Connecticut, **$1,500.**

Americans also developed a Windsor that swayed back and forth when the bottoms of its legs were cut off and notched slightly so that rockers could be joined to them. There are those who attribute this design to Benjamin Franklin. Others think a man wanted a comfortable seat for his wife while she tended their baby — and he made the rocking chair. The rocking style was widely accepted in the United States, but rejected by the English, who laughed at the idea of a chair that tilted back and forth.

This birdcage Windsor has carpet cutter rockers. 32″ high. In Illinois, **$400.**

35

A Windsor side chair with nicely tapered back spindles. 37½″ high. In Illinois, **$300.**

The maker's mark found beneath the seat of the Windsor side chair.

Consider other aspects in the construction of Windsors. The spindles in bow, arch, or loop backs differed and had to be the exact size to fit in their proper locations. Spindles were fashioned daintily to achieve a graceful appearance and yet offer strong support. Many tapered or slanted back slightly to increase comfort. Each part seemed to be designed to the exact size required for structural strength, but not any larger. The resulting Windsors were, as early advertisements stated, "Neat Assortments."

From the abundant American native forests, craftsmen selected hickory, ash, and white oak for loops, bows, or arches. These woods could be steamed and bent without breaking and would retain their shape.

Because the seats were contoured by hand-operated tools (an adz, gouging chisel, and block plane), a thick plank was required. As much as half of it might be taken off to form a "saddle" with a pommel in the middle and two equal hollows on each side into which the human body fit comfortably. Pine or birch was frequently used since either one is easier to shape than harder species, and one piece of wood was used to form the elliptical or shield-shaped seat.

Turned parts of maple, oak, ash, beech or birch were made on a foot treadle lathe. The chair's mixed woods did not show after being painted with such colors as green, black, red, white, yellow, or brown.

Some craftsmen favored combining unseasoned (not dried) and seasoned (dried) woods in such a manner that, as the fresh wood dried out, it gripped seasoned parts tightly. For example, as an unseasoned seat shrank after losing moisture, it would secure the previously seasoned spindles tightly. The many Windsors that have survived through the years attest to the skill of early craftsmen. The chairs were made to last.

It is natural that deviations in designs developed when machines replaced hand craftsmanship. Details that once created a gracious chair were neglected. An example is an eighteenth century low-back Windsor with gently tapered spindles. Versions of it were factory produced after the mid-1800s, and firemen were among those who found them useful. They were called Firehouse Windsors. The U-shaped arms, low back, slightly splayed legs, and a suggestion of a saddle seat were characteristics. The delicate spindles were replaced by thick, turned ones.

A similar type was used about 1875 when Mississippi River boat captains watched the swirling waters while seated in so-called captain's chairs that had a vague resemblance to the old low-back Windsors. The arms were a continuation of the back, curving down to be affixed to the front of the flat seat. Windsors were popular in hotels, clubs, offices, and homes and show how successfully the chairs were adapted to meet the needs of the day.

In spite of this, Windsor chairs, which reflect their delicate roots better than these two latter versions, have been produced continuously. They have retained the styling so sought-after in homes for many generations. Check a quality, American-made Windsor chair from the past for these features:

- Many finely shaped spindles (some say sticks).
- Legs with a pronounced splay (slant out).
- Shaped saddle seat (scooped out to fit the contour of the human body — rounded on each side and higher in the middle).
- Chamfered seat (bottom edge is bevelled — slants in).
- Sound construction (made to last).
- Made of various woods (and usually painted originally).
- Signs of hand workmanship (scribe lines, joints used, tool marks).
- Graceful, well balanced proportions.

Mississippi River boat personnel liked to sit in captain's chairs, circa 1875. 22″ arm to arm, 30″ high. In Illinois, **$95.**

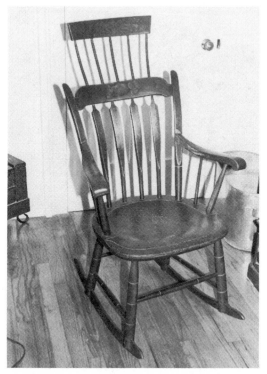

A pre-1830 New England example of an unusual arrow-back Windsor with a comb piece above the back rail. In Connecticut, **$250.**

Windsor armchair. 41″ high. In Iowa, **$495.**

Windsor arch-back chair with rush seat. 25″ arm to arm, 46″ high. In Illinois, **$200.**

Bar or captain's chair. In Illinois, **$115.**

Windsor captain's chair. 18½″ wide, 28½″ high. In Wisconsin, **$165.**

Captain's chair with cane bottom seat, 20″ arm to arm. 28½″ high. In Illinois, **$115.**

Windsor armchair, 23″ arm to arm, 32″ high. In Illinois, **$135.**

# 3  Well and cistern days

**A**t present, in order to conserve water, restaurants are not supposed to place glasses on the table unless diners request them. Years ago, water also caused concern. Settlements were established where a supply was available. Streams provided this body-sustaining liquid. If a river permitted travel by boat or yielded fish for food, that was an added plus.

Adult sized sickroom armchair with stenciled, splat back, rolled arms, ship scene on top rail. 23″ arm to arm, 47″ high. In Illinois, **$175.**

Homesteaders dug wells. Wooden buckets were attached to long ropes, and later, pumps were used to bring the precious liquid to the surface. A tin cup hung nearby so that all who were thirsty could drink from this communal source. For all needs, water was carried into the house.

Before pipes brought water gushing into homes, many special furnishings provided water-related needs. Some were for emergencies, sickroom, child training, or nocturnal musts when a privy answered the question "How do you spell relief?" (Other names for it were "necessary," "outhouse," or "backhouse.") Here are some substitutes for this room of the crescent moon. (Really, many were designed with a small moon-shaped, cutout air vent.)

An adult-size necessary chair could serve the ill and the old. The stenciled designs remain distinct with flowers on the back splat and a ship scene on the top rail. A round lid with a sunken handle could be removed from the seat.

Washstands often kept covered chamber pots handy, but they usually peeked out from a hidden spot under the bed. Aah — all the comforts of home. Wash bowls and pitchers were also included in chamber sets, and are the usual surviving units. Sometimes, they are used to hold plants, today, but an inner liner should be inserted to protect them from damaging residue. People are cautioned not to store or pour punch from the

Washstand with hole in top for bowl and shelf with one drawer. 17″ wide, 14″ deep, 34″ high. In Illinois, **$255.**

Common washstand with towel bar ends. 25″ wide, 17″ deep, 28½″ high. In Wisconsin, **$295.**

pitchers. They were not made to hold beverages, and the body or glaze could contain ingredients that are harmful to the health.

Years ago, personal bathing was done in the privacy of the bedchamber, and furniture to store needed items was standard equipment. Common hand-washing stands had a shelf at the base. Some had towel bars on which to hang supplies. If a stand had a hole in the middle of the top, it accommodated a bowl graciously.

Commode washstands combined doors or a door with drawers. The lidded slop pot, into which waste was dumped to be transported to the backhouse during daylight hours, was headquartered behind the closed doors.

Pine commode, 24″ wide, 21½″ deep, 28″ high. In Illinois, **$245.**

Lift-top oak commode with drawer on left and fake drawer on right. 28″ wide, 18½″ deep, 31½″ high. In Pennsylvania, **$295.**

Cherry bureau commode with towel bar ends, ogee top drawer. 37″ wide, 15½″ deep, 35½″ high. In Illinois, **$345.**

Recently, it was almost pack-up time at a large city flea market when a young man approached a couple who seemed interested in one of his pieces. He appeared desperate to make a sale. "That washstand is solid walnut," he said. "It's too bad someone added hinges, but the top could be nailed down again. I could give you a nice price reduction. With a little work, you'd have a beautiful piece of furniture." The couple gently informed him it was a lift-top commode and had been made so that its top flipped up on hinges. The bowl was placed on a step inside, and a tall pitcher was in the low section behind the false drawer. Rings from water stains frequently outlined where they were placed.

Bureau commodes are small, three-drawer chests. A retractable rod that pulled out of a hole in the side was often available to provide supplies, or often there might be towel bars at the ends. Keeping people neat was a major purpose of bedroom furniture.

Next in the exploration of a house without plumbing, consider the porch. When the noon dinner bell clanged "Come and get it," the men and boys charged toward the water bench, which was a warm weather inhabitant of the back porch or yard. Washcloths were not required. Water was ladled from a bucket into a basin. A man lathered his hands generously with soap before scrubbing his face and neck. He shook off excess moisture, rinsed in a similar hand-rubbing manner as he splashed generously. After running damp fingers through his hair and drying on a group towel, he was ready to eat. That essential washbench grew weathered and battered as it served the farm workers.

The kitchen had a space reserved for family ablutions. It could be a shelf with a washbasin perched upon it and a small mirror hanging above. A rod for a roller towel and a metal comb case were near. A towel bar could be combined with a cabinet in which toilet articles were kept.

Pine water bench. 29″ wide, 20″ deep, 30″ high. In Illinois, **$135.**

Towel bar roller has pine back, maple roller. 21¼″ wide, 6″ deep. In Illinois, **$60.**

Taking a full bath was a Saturday night ritual in most homes. A tub was dragged into the middle of the kitchen and filled with water heated on the cookstove. Each person took a turn. Everyone had to be clean to attend church Sunday morning. The last bather was responsible for the final clean-up job before he put the tub away until the next Saturday. If the same tub served for washing clothes, it could be left out for this Monday chore. The women and girls sometimes boiled the clothes in a large boiler set on the stove top and rubbed them on scrub boards to get the dirt out. It was a tiring, day-long chore, and little washbenches held the necessary tubs.

Pine spice cabinet with towel bar roller. 19½″ wide, 6½″ deep, 25″ high. In Illinois, **$175.**

Pine washbench, 39″ wide, 13½″ deep, 14″ high. In Illinois, **$65.**

Washtub, sometimes used as a butter bucket. 24″ diameter, 11″ high, stand 18″ high, paddle 41″ long. In Louisiana, **$125.**

Pine dry sink, chamfered door panels, paneled ends, 40½″ wide, 18½″ deep, 33½″ high, 7″ from well to top of back rail. In Connecticut, **$750.**

There was one special cabinet that might be a part of the kitchen furnishings. It was lined with zinc and referred to as a "dry sink." Here all tasks that involved water could be completed. Cleaning vegetables, peeling apples, or washing dishes would not harm its metal-protected surface. There might be a hole through which the waste drained into a bucket beneath. When full, its contents could be dumped outside. Some say the word "sink" was derived from the slurring of the work "zinc" — in any case, it was handy equipment in a kitchen that lacked plumbing facilities.

Of course, a pail with a long handled dipper in it was standard equipment. When someone was asked, "May I get you a drink?" an affirmative response elicited a cup of cold well water, pulled up from deep in the earth.

Pine washstand, 22″ wide, 18″ deep, 29″ high. In Illinois, **$175.**

45

Pennsylvania-type pine washstand with hole in the top. 28½″ wide, 17½″ deep, 32½″ high. In Illinois, **$195.**

Pine washstand with candleholders in corners. 17″ wide, 14″ deep, 28½″ high. In Connecticut, **$175.**

Common washstand in pine with towel bar ends. In Connecticult, **$95.**

Commode washstand in pine. 30″ wide, 15½″ deep, 28″ high. In Illinois, **$325.**

Poplar commode washstand, with marble top and splashback. 29″ wide, 17″ deep, 31½″ high. In Illinois, **$700.**

Commode washstand in butternut. 30½″ wide, 15″ deep, 31″ high, splashback 5″. In Wisconsin, **$265.**

Pine commode. 22″ wide, 13½″ deep, 31½″ high, with side rails extending 2″ beyond top. In Illinois, **$350.**

Commode washstand in pine with candle stands on back rail; once a part of a painted and stenciled three-piece cottage set. In Illinois, **$265.**

47

Pine commode. 32″ wide, 19″ deep, 29″ high. In Illinois, **$225.**

Lift-top pine commode, 29½″ wide, 17½″ deep, 32½″ high. In Illinois, **$310.**

Lift-top poplar commode with breadboard ends on top, no drawers. In Illinois, **$225.**

Walnut bucket bench. 32″ wide, 6″ deep top shelf, 12½″ deep bottom shelf, 42″ high. In Nebraska, **$395.**

Bucket bench, pine stripped to red. 34½″ wide, 11½″ deep, 42″ high. In Ohio, **$375.**

Pine water bench with shelves worn thin from use. In Illinois, **$160.**

Pine dry sink. 46″ wide, 19″ deep, 33″ to well, 53″ overall height. In Maryland, **$975.**

Oak dry sink. 45″´ wide, 18″ deep, 32″ to well, 49″ overall height. In Illinois, **$650.**

Zinc lined pine dry sink with walnut panel in doors. 60″ wide, 21″ deep, 31½″ to well, 45″ overall height. In Illinois, **$550.** Lamps from left to right: pewter time lamp, silver-over-copper lacemaker's lamp, whey butter lamp, betty lamp and tidy stand, camphine and pewter time lamps.

Pine dry sink, wainscot front. 32½″ wide, 16″ deep, 32″ high. In Illinois, **$250.**

Dry sink in pine. 41½″ wide, 26″ deep, 49″ high. In New York, **$345.**

Cherry dry sink with unusual drawer and door construction, bun feet. 39½″ wide, 19½″ deep, 36″ high. In Iowa, **$675.**

Zinc lined walnut dry sink. 38″ wide, 15½″ deep, 27″ high. In Illinois, **$600.**

Pine dry sink, wainscot front. 36″ wide, 16″ deep, 29″ high. In Illinois, **$350.**

Pine dry sink with ample storage space. 38¼″ wide, 16¼″ deep, 33″ high. In Illinois, **$675.**

Pine dry sink. 45″ wide, 19″ deep, 40″ high. In Illinois, **$525.**

Pine dry sink. 42½″ wide, 19½″ deep, 31½″ high. In Illinois, **$475.**

Pine dry sink with nickel-over-copper drainboard, back, and drain tub, circa 1920. 29½″ wide, 20½″ deep, 30″ high. In Illinois, **$150.**

Pine washbench with shelf, bootjack legs. 33½″ wide, 14″ deep, 18″ high. In Illinois, **$125.**

# 4   What's cookin'?

**A** kitchen's the homey spot in the house. In pioneer days, a fireplace was used for cooking tasks plus providing heat and light. Today, with separate rooms for sitting, recreation, sleeping, and bathing, it is hard to remember that people frequently had one main room and a loft, especially when their circumstances were meager. Essentials hung from pegs or nails on the wall, and the hearth was cluttered with iron pots, Dutch ovens, copper kettles, stirrers, strainers, and dippers. Dried herbs and onions dangled from the ceiling. Clutter was everywhere, but not much space or time was wasted by frugal families. Later, a narrow chimney cupboard helped store materials.

A cleverly designed unit was the settle or chair or bench table. The top was flipped up to reveal a seat. The wide expanse of wood of the flipped-up top helped keep drafts off human backs as the sitter cozied up to the fireplace. This piece could serve as a table, a place to sit, and a storage place if it had a lift-lid compartment. Other plain benches also were available for family use.

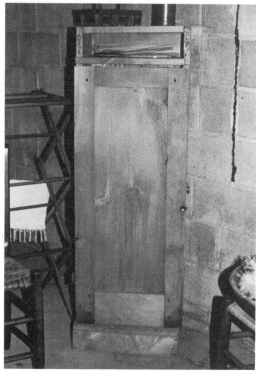

Chimney cupboard in pine with pegged doors has open shelf on top. 17½″ wide, 10½″ deep, 53″ high. In Illinois, **$175.**

Settle or hutch table, pine and poplar, early shoe feet, lift lid seat. Top 48″ wide, 30″ deep, 28½″ high when a table. In Connecticut, **$1,400.**

Pine washbench with bootjack legs. 54″ wide, 14″ deep, 19″ high. In Illinois, **$185.** Also, three legged milk stool. 14¼″ wide, 7″ deep, 13″ high, **$35.** Rolling pin, **$25.** Wooden tub, **$65.** Peel, above bench on wall, 67½″ long, **$75.**

Mortar and pestle with trace of red paint on outside, incised lines, vertical age split. 5½″ diameter, 7½″ high. In Illinois, **$70.**

Since home baking was the norm, a fireplace might have an auxiliary hole for this purpose. A peel was a long, shovel-like tool that was used to put food in the oven or take it out. Pans were placed on the peel's flat surface and inserted into the heated space. A slight joggle slipped them into the oven safely so the peel could be extracted. The baked items were removed by sliding this tool underneath and lifting the pans out.

Since farms tended to be self-sufficient units, homemade articles abounded. The word "treen" — derived from tree with an "n" added — refers to small woodenware. Bowls, scoops, plates, cooking spoons, and mortars and pestles, were some items a man made out of wood for his home. A figural scoop of the late 1700s or early 1800s that required more dexterity and imagination than an ordinary type had a hooked end vaguely resembling a horse's head.

Maple scoop, eighteenth century with horse's head figural handle. 9″ long, 4½″ wide. In New York, **$120.**

A crudely fashioned wooden butter worker helped a housewife of the past as she made a golden spread from the cream produced by the family's cows.

Butter worker of hand-hewn pine. 30″ wide, 16″ deep, 5″ high. In Illinois, **$145.**

Betty lamp with lid. In Connecticut, **$225.**

Dovetailed pine doughbox has maple legs added to make end table. 37″ wide, 16″ deep, 31″ high. In Illinois, **$325.**

Hand-wrought iron articles are old. Lighting was a problem. Perhaps, that is why people were up at daybreak and went to bed at dark. Lamps of Ben Franklin's days provided feeble lights. They smoked. They smelled. Iron examples were hand-shaped by tradesmen who spent years in apprenticeship. One lamp was called a betty. This was a step up from a crusie because it provided a tube for the wick to sit in, not merely a font for the fuel and a wick. It dates to the late 1600s or the early 1700s. Some sources say the lamp's name is derived from "betying," a Colonial colloquialism for leavings and/or crude fat. Tin examples are rarer than iron ones, but reproductions run rampant. Irregularities and roughness should be apparent in a lamp wrought by hand — but these can be faked. Imports from such places as Mexico have that old appearance. Be wary.

As the years passed, the importance of the fireplace diminished. A stove burned coal, corncobs, or wood. Women knew how much fuel was required to elevate the oven temperature for pie baking or bread making, and delectable cooking smells permeated the room. Families tended to be large in number, and with the hired help, plenty of bread had to be available. Large batches of bread could be mixed in dough boxes. The lid provided a space for kneading and shaping. Some were on legs, but many were portable, tabletop models. Collectors have added to some tabletop styles, and they now serve as end tables.

If a young lad appreciated the hot fresh bread or the pies his mother baked, he had to help make them possible. The woodbox continually needed refilling. It was his task to haul in armloads of short-cut logs. An older brother might be the chopper and splitter who cut the logs to the size the stove could accommodate. Cooperation kept the home a united unit.

Special cupboards were available to meet varied needs. Meal bins held wheat and rye flour as well as cornmeal. The styling could be plain or fancy. A dough cupboard with a cylinder top to hide a pull-out work surface fits in the latter category. It is a contrast to a primitive backless cupboard or an early 1800s corner pantry.

Pine woodbox with lift lid, slant top. 14½″ wide, 17″ deep, 24″ high at front. In Illinois, **$155.**

Dough cupboard in oak with cylinder top. 34″ wide, 21″ deep at base, 48″ high. In Ohio, **$675.**

Dough cupboard shown with lid raised exposing draw-out board on which the dough raised.

Backless open cupboard in pine with replaced drawer in right-hand vertical support. 41″ wide, 14″ deep, 53″ high. In Wisconsin, **$365.**

Pine corner pantry, 45½″ wide, 23″ deep, 53″ high. In Illinois, **$650.**

The 1800s was the era of the cupboard. Pie safes had a variety of punched-tin panels. Geometric or star designs were prominent. The holes were punched in or out. The tin panels served a dual purpose. They permitted air to circulate to retard molding of freshly baked products and, at the same time, prevented flies or rodents from reaching the foods. In this sense, tins really did function as safes.

Since the women and girls worked diligently all summer to preserve surplus food for winter use, certain cupboards whose contents glowed with grape, peach, strawberry, or apple colors were known as jelly cupboards. After long hours over a hot cookstove, the ladies filled the shelves with sweet goodness, especially appreciated when spread on home-baked bread.

Pie safe in pine and poplar with unique door and drawer construction, punched and pressed tin door panels. 40″ wide, 17½″ deep, 54″ high. In Pennsylvania, **$450.**

Jelly cupboard in poplar and maple has molded doors, plank ends. 44″ wide, 16½″ deep, 53″ high. In Illinois, **$365.**

Cupboards may be squat or tall, wide or skinny. They may have four doors, two, or one. But if wooden and enclosed, they are commonly called closed cupboards. The old ones were put together with pegs, square nails, and special joiner's joints. The doors attest to the work of hand planes because edges are uneven and chamfered (bevelled).

An Ohio dealer recently displayed a cupboard that is typical of those made by men of German descent. Only a narrow space is allotted where cups are to be placed. Wide spaces are reserved for large plates, so the shelves are arranged in an uneven pattern to meet these requirements.

Two-piece closed cupboard in pine and poplar with chamfered upper door panels. 50¼″ wide, 21″ deep at step back. 75½″ high. Notice Bennington-type ware with Rockingham glaze in cupboard. In Ohio, **$685.**

Walnut closed cupboard, originally one piece, but converted to two for ease in moving, typically German wide spaced shelves for plates and narrow spaced ones for cups. 45″ wide, 20½″ deep, 31½″ high base; 13½″ deep, 45″ high top section. In Ohio, **$1,200.**

"Tramp art" type small cabinet used as end table by chair. 18″ wide, 10″ deep, 19½″ high. In Illinois, **$150.**

Corner cupboard has pegged door, 30″ wide, 18″ deep, 48½″ high; open-back shelf, original black paint, hand planed shelves. 21″ wide, 10″ deep, 39½″ high. In Illinois, **$700.**

The owner of a tiny home-crafted cabinet used it as an end table near a chair. It was put together crudely with scraps, including leather thong hinges and a board on top that said "St. Louis, Mo." The cigar box drawers are molded. Its owner described it as a "tramp art sort of piece."

Often, a corner piece combined two cupboard styles. The top shelf never had a back, and it was designed to hang in a corner or sit on the floor. It rested comfortably in pickaback fashion on top of an enclosed base corner cupboard to make an attractive marriage.

Someone remarked recently that she would like to buy a corner cupboard. "But I don't have any corners to put it in," she added, wisely. That's because many factors must be considered before a cupboard can be backed into an existing space. Will the cupboard block windows, doors, outlets, heat ducts, or air conditioning units? Will it protrude too far? Will it be a safe distance from a fireplace or heating stove? Corner cupboards are difficult to accommodate.

Cupboards with open top shelves or glass enclosed ones are airy in appearance, and they serve their owners well by supplying storage or display space.

"Where or where has my little top gone?" This might be the wail of a base made about the turn of the century. It has a flour bin on one side and a drawer on the other. A rail has been added around the top. Even though it is cobbled, it remains a useful piece. The owner of another cupboard should win an award in a "you name it" contest. She dubs it the "Stuff Cabinet" because someone once kept a lot of stuff in it. After all, that's why cupboards were made.

Poplar corner cupboard. 41″ wide, 19″ deep, 81″ high. In Illinois, **$650.**

Maple cupboard. 38″ wide, 17″ deep, 79½″ high. In Illinois, **$400.** Cranberry scoop at cupboard base is used for magazines, **$115.**

Kitchen base cupboard in pine with pull-out flour bin at left. 43½″ wide, 19½″ deep, 33½″ high. In Illinois, **$245.**

What's a kitchen without spicy odors drifting from it? Perhaps, that's why oldtime kitchens had spice cabinets hanging around. Six are shown in this book, and no two are alike. They range from a primitive type in a box cupboard to one with porcelain drawer pulls surrounded by a design of spokes. (Wagon wheels?) Usually, the names of spices were glued on each drawer front. Other styles had brass tags on the drawers to list the spices within. Most cabinets were made entirely of wood. Recently, one made of tin highlighted an antiquer's display. The cabinet, with two drawers below, was quite at home. It was in the company of an apple butter paddle, a bread board, and a bedside table fashioned from a mixture of woods. Alongside was a longhorn cheese mold that had been filled, tamped down, and left overnight. Its rings then were removed to release the cheese that had formed a skin while in the mold.

Pine kitchen cabinet, called a "Stuff Cabinet" because lots of stuff was kept in it. 43½″ wide, 20½″ deep, 57″ high. In Pennsylvania, **$375.**

Spice cabinet. In Illinois, **$105.**

Spice cabinet with brass marker plates. 7″ wide, 2½″ deep, 11″ high. In Illinois, **$92.50.**

Walnut spice cabinet. 8″ wide, 4″ deep, 10″ high. In Illinois, **$150.**

Spice cabinet in pine with butternut drawer fronts. 7½″ wide, 5½″ deep, 12″ high. In Iowa, **$165.**

Ten-drawer spice cabinet built into cupboard base. 9½″ wide, 7″ deep, 25″ high. In Indiana, **$95.**

Tin spice cabinet with eight drawers, two bins. 11″ wide, 5½″ deep, 17½″ high. In Illinois, **$175.** Bedside table, mixed woods, 22½″ wide, 15″ deep, 29″ high, **$95.** Cheese mold. 39½″ high, 4¼″ diameter, **$110.**

Corner shelf is a modern primitive made with round nails and corrugated fasteners. 28″ high. In Illinois, **$75.**

A recently constructed primitive illustrates rustic corner shelves. The used boards were hammered together to fit a special area. They may have been retrieved from a farm shed or barn. Corrugated fasteners and round nails added assurance that "it is not old." Primitive, yes; old, no!

A kitchen of the 1840s needed a dry sink for washing purposes. And this one was made with diligence, with mortise and tenon doors, a chamfered bottom on the drawer, and square nails. A kraut cutter often hung above it.

Pine dry sink with mortise and tenon doors, chamfered drawer bottoms, square nails, circa 1840. 44½″ wide, 17″ deep, 34½″ high. In Illinois, **$525.**

Dropleaf table, maple, circa 1910. 42″ wide, 26″ deep, 29½″ high, each leaf 12″ wide. In Illinois, **$245.**

In the past, country kitchens had generous tables around which the whole family sat. The maple table shown in this chapter is from the early 1900s. Naturally, the young lad thinks it's time to be fed. The work table shown has a zinc top to withstand water. The table also is circa 1900.

Zinc top work table, red paint evidence, circa 1900. 36″ wide, 23½″ deep, 30½″ high. It would make a good potter's table. In Ohio, **$225.**

An older person who liked to do small household tasks in order to feel useful sat in a small rocker frequently as she shelled peas, snapped the ends off beans, or peeled apples. Other types and styling of chairs were used in early kitchens. Several are pictured here and more will be found in the next chapter.

Maple and pine rocking chair, rolled front and back seat. 37″ high. In Wisconsin, **$295.**

Set of six kitchen chairs, mixed woods which is typical of most chairs. 31″ high. In Illinois, **$650.**

Kitchen chair. 33″ high. In Illinois, **$75.**

Kitchen chair, 32″ high. In Illinois, **$65.**

Maple kitchen chair. 35½″ high. In Illinois, **$65.**

It must have been hard to leave the kitchen on a cold winter night in the North. There would be a fast dash up the stairs to the unheated bedchamber in order to hop into a cold bed. If a bed warmer (hot coals in a long handled, lidded pan) were first rubbed over the sleeping surface, the transition was easier. In the morning, it probably took a few moments of indecision before one braved the cold by thrusting back the quilts. Children often grabbed garments and raced to dress behind the warm kitchen stove. Yes, the kitchen definitely was the center for family living.

Today's country kitchens catch snatches of life in the past and cast a romantic aura over the belongings of former generations. It is a pleasant way to teach youth about their heritage by exposing them to items their great grandma might have had.

Stenciled chair, set of six. 33″ high. In Illinois, each **$175.**

Pine chimney cupboard with secret compartment at base. 15¼″ wide, 15″ deep, 62″ high. In Ohio, **$245.**

Walnut chimney cupboard. 28″ wide, 14½″ deep, 53½″ high. In Illinois, **$325.**

Pine chimney cupboard. 18″ wide, 17½″ deep, 64″ high. In Illinois, **$280.**

Walnut settle table with lift-lid seat, scalloped apron. 43½″ wide, 21″ deep, 17″ to seat, 55″ overall height. In Ohio, **$625.**

Chair-table. 48″ diameter, 24″ wide, 26″ deep base section. In Iowa, **$950.**

Pine dough tray on legs. 34″ wide, 16″ deep, 31″ high. In Illinois, **$175.** Butter churn on top, **$125.** Coffee grinder, **$75.** Small doll trunk, **$75.**

Dough tray with dovetailed ends has glass topped well holding miniature furniture. 32″ wide, 15½″ deep, 16½″ high. In Pennsylvania, **$350.**

Pine dough box, nailed construction. 34½″ wide, 15½″ deep, 31″ high. In Illinois, **$325.**

Pine woodbox. 23½″ wide, 19½″ deep at base, 41½″ high. In Illinois, **$135.**

Pine woodbox. 31″ wide, 20½″ high, 35″ high. In Nebraska, **$275.** Shaped chopping board, **$46.**

Woodbox-cupboard combination in pine. 46″ wide, 17½″ deep, 39″ high on woodbox side. In Indiana, **$400.**

72

Closed cupboard with front doors removed, punched tin side panels. 37″ wide, 15½″ deep, 69″ high. In Illinois, **$375.**

Walnut pie safe with punched tin door panels, pegged construction. 40½″ wide, 17″ deep, 60″ high. In Virginia, **$475.**

Food cupboard has screened doors and side panels, mortise and tenon door, pegged, square nails. 52″ wide, 18″ deep, 34½″ high. In Illinois, **$375.**

Pine and poplar pie safe has screening in doors and side panels. 50″ wide, 17½″ deep, 52″ high. In Wisconsin, **$325.**

Pine pie safe with cathedral design tin panels. 40½″ wide, 17½″ deep, 55″ high. In Illinois, **$650.**

Pine pie safe with cherry base, walnut top, six punched tin panels. 37½″ wide, 17″ deep, 54″ high. In Illinois, **$850.**

Pine and poplar pie safe with punched tin star design. 44″ wide, 16″ deep, 72″ high. In Illinois, **$385.**

74

Pie safe with floral motif punched in tin side panels. In Iowa, **$375.**

Pie safe, plank ends, star-within-star surrounded by four stars pattern in punched tin door panels. 41″ wide, 15″ deep, 56″ high. In Illinois, **$375.**

Pie safe, heart and star punched tin end panels. 42½″ wide, 17″ deep, 52″ high. In Illinois, **$275.**

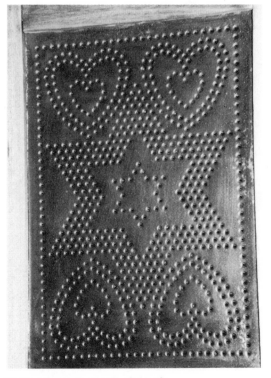

Punched tin panels on ends of pie safe.

Pie safe in ash with two round air vents on each end. 39½″ wide, 15¼″ deep, 50″ high. In Maryland, **$395.**

Walnut jelly cupboard. 41″ wide, 15½″ deep, 50½″ high. In Iowa, **$625.**

Jelly cupboard. 43″ wide, 18½″ deep, 51½″ high. In Illinois, **$375.**

Poplar jelly cupboard, doorknobs missing; label on back reads, "St. Louis Refrigerator & Wooden Gutter Co." 38½″ wide, 16½″ deep, 64″ high. In Illinois, **$395.**

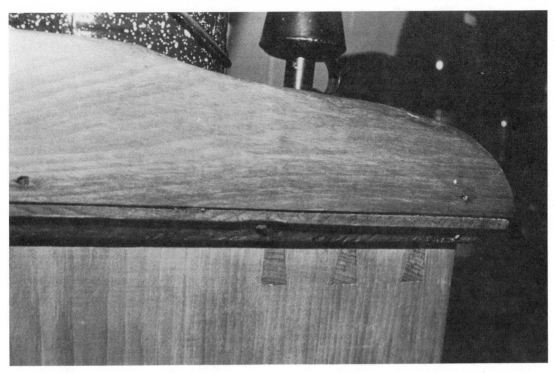

Dovetail construction shows how side is secured to top of jelly cupboard.

Walnut jelly cupboard. 33½″ wide, 17½″ deep, 41″ high. In Illinois, **$375.**

Pine jelly cupboard. 25″ wide, 9″ deep, 31″ high. In Nebraska, **$265.**

Pine commode washstand. 30″ wide, 17½″ deep, 31″ high. In Ohio, **$195.**

Pine and poplar jelly cupboard. 43″ wide, 18½″ deep, 39″ high. In Illinois, **$255.**

Pine and poplar jelly cupboard. 42½″ wide, 18½″ deep, 42½″ high, 7″ rail. In Maryland, **$385.**

Pine cabinet base with inscribed door decorations. 38″ wide, 18½″ deep, 38″ high. In Illinois, **$350.**

78

Closed cupboard in chestnut. 36″ wide, 17½″ deep, 72″ high. In Connecticut, **$550.**

Butternut closed cupboard. 74½″ wide, 14½″ deep, 76½″ high. In Wisconsin, **$895.**

Small workstand with lift top, bootjack legs. 16½″ wide, 11″ deep, 18½″ high. In Illinois, **$150.**

Pine storage cabinet with glass doors. 19″ wide, 19″ deep, 32½″ high. In Illinois, **$265.**

Poplar storage cabinet. 19½″ wide, 15½″ deep, 31″ high. In Illinois, **$125.**

Cupboard base, wainscoting. 30″ wide, 14″ deep, 32″ high. In Illinois, **$175.**

Utility cupboard used in barn. 16½″ wide, 10″ deep, 26″ high. In Illinois, **$95.**

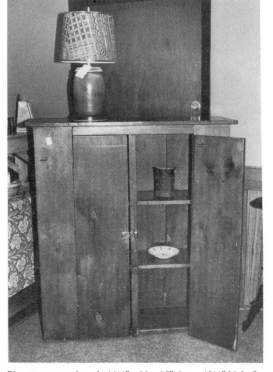

Pine storage cupboard. 44½″ wide, 15″ deep, 49½″ high. In Wisconsin, **$185.**

Medicine-type cabinet. 11″ wide, 6″ deep, 20″ high. In Illinois, **$85.**

Utility cupboard in pine. 13″ wide, 5½″ deep, 19½″ high to shelf, overall height 30½″. In Illinois, **$125.**

Closed corner cupboard. 52″ wide, 17½″ deep, 77″ high. In Illinois, **$900.**

One-piece closed cupboard used on a Michigan farm. 40″ wide, 14½″ deep, 75″ high. In Michigan, **$485.**

Pine open cupboard with door and drawer at base. 32″ wide, 12½″ deep, 69″ high. In Nebraska, **$950.** Country quilt on first shelf, 72″ x 81″, **$125.** Milking stool, **$48.**

Pine cupboard sandwiched between two drawers. 34″ wide, 13″ deep, 42½″ high. In Illinois, **$325.**

Pine cupboard with glass doors and drawer at base. 35″ wide, 13″ deep, 60½″ high. In Illinois, **$225.**

Two-piece pine cupboard. 42½″ wide, 18″ deep, 84″ high. In Illinois, **$695.**

Pine cupboard. 42″ wide, 14″ deep, 72″ high. In Illinois, **$600.**

Pine cupboard (kitchen cabinet), circa 1900. 43″ wide, 21″ deep, 82″ high. In Indiana, **$695.**

Pine and poplar closed cupboard with large work surface, doors on all three sides, and pull-out breadboard. 37″ wide, 28″ deep, 60″ high. In Illinois, **$650.**

Walnut jelly cupboard. 41½″ wide, 11″ deep, 47″ high. In Illinois, **$210.**

Cupboard. 28″ wide, 13″ deep, 30¼″ high. In Illinois, **$210.**

Pine cupboard. 37½″ wide, 15½″ deep, 38½″ high. In Illinois, **$295.**

# 5 Come sup with me

et's start in the dining room with reflections about a slat back, rush seat chair. The legs were cut off to stumps for a purpose. The chair was flipped over on its back and a toddler was supported while he learned to walk. The wee one scooted the chair across the floor boards. This wore down the finials on the underside. There must have been a batch of young children because the area removed by friction is generous in size. Besides the crooked construction, the scribed guidelines are an additional sign of hand work.

So far, a red painted, brightly stenciled chair with its natural rush seat has defied identification. Could it be a kin to the mid-1900s chairs that were whittled by a Missouri hill man and rushed with native swamp reed because a woman needed a set? It's fun to wonder.

Chair with rush seat. In Connecticut, **$125.**

Stenciled chair, set of eight, twentieth century. In Connecticut, the set, **$550.**

Chair with rush seat, circa 1830. In Pennsylvania, **$85.**

Stenciled chair from Ohio, circa 1850, needs rush seat replaced. In Pennsylvania, **$45.**

And here's another family tale. A blind great-grandfather always recognized a chair as his own because it had a small nick in the back that he could run his hands over. It dates to 1820-1830 and has a simplicity of line that's pleasing.

# Hitchcock Chairs

Lambert Hitchcock receives the credit for introducing factory methods in the production of furniture. Since his fancy, painted side chairs sold well, others copied them. All chairs of this type are now listed under the generic title of Hitchcock chairs. Stacks of legs, backs, rungs, and seats are not as bulky to package as ready-to-use chairs, so Hitchcock shipped his products unassembled.

Hitchcock began his factory in about 1820, and generally his company name is stenciled on the back edge of the seat. The markings from 1825-29 read "L. Hitchcock, Hitchcocks-ville, Conn. Warranted." The name "Hitchcock, Alford, & Co., Hitchcocks-ville, Conn., Warranted" was used during the time when a relative by marriage was associated with the firm. After the partnership was dissolved, the label from 1843-52 was "Lambert Hitchcock, Unionville, Conn." The labels should always be preserved.

The top rail frequently featured a wooden pillow or a roll. A wide back slat was bold with colorful flowers, fruits, or an eagle. Some were artificially grained to resemble expensive rosewood. Current owners tend to strip these pre-1850 chairs of their worn dark paint with its faded stenciling, and purists find this practice disturbing. They want their chair as is. The circa 1850 chair from Ohio shown here should have a rush seat. With its rolled top rail and wide slat, it closely resembles chairs from the Hitchock factory. These chairs follow styles popularized by the English cabinetmaker, Thomas Sheraton.

Notice the shape and slant of the front rung on the fancy side chair in this chapter. Examples such as these are often designated "Baltimore Hitchcocks."

Baltimore Hitchcock chair. In Connecticut, **$90.**

Side chair, repainted and decaled to approximate original look. In Pennsylvania, **$125.**

Chairs with back spindles that are flattened and have a pointed shape are known as arrow backs. The ends of the upright supports on this chair are "rabbit ears" that extend above the top rail. The one-piece board seat is called a plank bottom. This chair has been repainted, but closely resembles the original finish.

What's a dining room without tables? A fine example of a harvest table is included in the second chapter with Windsor chairs all around it. An open mortise and tenon joint on the base support shows clearly.

Nun's dining table with twelve drawers for plates and table service for each nun; of maple, elm, ash. 10′ long, 2′11″ wide, 31″ high. Benches accommodated nuns as they ate. In Iowa, **$650.**

Pine open cupboard, one piece with chamfered doors. 51″ wide, 20″ deep, 41½″ to top of base, 83½″ overall height. In Illinois, **$1,400.**

Surely, she's just joshing, but the owner of a nun's table claims she purchased it at an auction and almost lost her happy home as a result. "I thought my husband was going to walk out on me," she recalled. She sent him to get it from a nearby town. No way would its bulk squeeze into a pickup truck. It hung over the outside edge. She also had not checked to see whether her room could receive such a lengthy resident, and he was sure they'd never be able to maneuver it into position.

The nun's table came from a convent in Dubuque, Iowa, and was used by a dozen nuns who sat prayerfully around it. Each nun had a drawer to store her dinner service, which she drew forth at mealtimes. The table has a maple top. There are five elm or ash legs, with one support in the middle. Probably, benches were the original seats.

A one-piece cupboard is hard to manipulate when it's huge and heavy. It goes by various names such as hutch cupboard, dresser, or open cupboard. With any of these names, it remains an attractive piece for displaying china.

A hand-made, pegged cupboard, basically of plain pine, has an odd feature. It's a drawer at the peak of the cornice. The owner referred to it as a recipe drawer, but that seems an unlikely use when the location is beyond easy reach. Maybe, important personal papers were kept out-of-sight there.

Slat back, woven seat chair. In Pennsylvania, pair, **$55.**

Pine cupboard with small drawer in top cornice. 43½″ wide, 18″ deep, 78″ high. In Iowa, **$750.**

Windsor-type chair with black paint, stencil on back rail, and gold trim. In Iowa, **$125.**

Black plank seat fancy chairs with stenciling and gold trim. In Illinois, each **$90.**

Fancy, painted side chairs with unusual half-arrow spindles and diamond center front rungs. In Ohio, set of four, **$425.**

Convex, bowed rung side chair, black with gold trimming. In Connecticut, **$90.**

Side chair with rush seat. In Connecticut, **$125.**

Plank seat side chair. In Pennsylvania, **$60.**

Pine dining table, molded edges on top, front and side drawer. 60″ long, 35″ deep, 31″ high. In Iowa, **$800.**

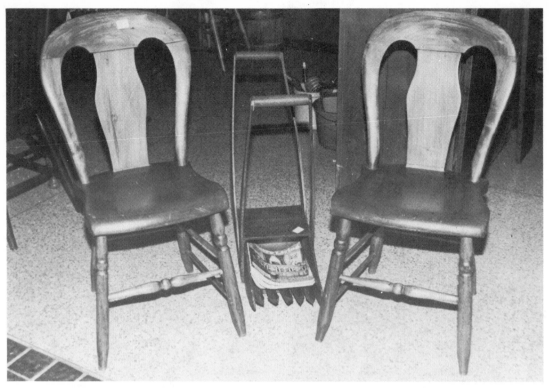

Balloon backed splat back chairs. In Illinois, each **$100.**

Pine store display table. 8′ long, 2′ deep, 30½″ high. In Illinois, **$325.**

Walnut dining table, square turned legs. 62″ wide, 28½″ deep, 28½″ high. In Illinois, **$400.**

Plank top dining table, plain legs, 7′1″ long, 39½″ deep, 29½″ high. In Connecticut, not priced.

Dropleaf cherry dining table. 42½″ wide, 19″ deep, 28″ high, drop leaves 13″. In Pennsylvania, **$350.**

Dropleaf cherry dining table. 42½″ wide, 17½″ deep, 29″ high, drop leaves 11½″. In Pennsylvania, **$375.**

Maple cupboard, one piece. 48″ wide, 18″ deep, 40½″ to step, 78″ overall height. In Illinois, **$950.**

Cherry cupboard. 48½″ wide, 18″ deep, 81″ high. In Illinois, **$850.**

Closed two-piece corner cupboard in walnut with molded, cathedral type panels in doors shows the craftsman skill of an experienced journeyman. 48″ wide, 26½″ deep, 85″ high. In Iowa, **$2,450.**

Cupboard in walnut and butternut. 40½″ wide, 18″ deep at base, 11½″ deep at top, 89″ high. In Illinois, **$750.**

Open corner cupboard in pine with some vestiges of red paint. 54″ wide, 25″ deep, 80″ high. In Pennsylvania, **$650.**

One-piece walnut cupboard, circa 1820-1850. 49½″ wide, 18¼″ deep, 82½″ high. In Ohio, **$1,500.**

Oak and maple kitchen cupboard. 39″ wide, 16½″ deep, 73″ high. In Ohio, **$325.**

Dry sink, poplar and oak. 48″ wide, 18½″ deep, 47″ high. In Illinois, **$575.**

Ice cream table, in Iowa, **$150.** Heart back chair, **$50.** Club back chair, **$75.**

Pine cupboard with one drawer, two doors. In Connecticut, **$425.**
Pennsylvania patchwork quilt, late 1800s, 6′4″ by 7′, **$435.**

Pine jelly cupboard. 41½″ wide, 15″ deep, 51″ high. In Iowa, **$300.** Diamond Dye cabinet, 21″ wide, 10″ deep, 30″ high, **$300.**
Butter churn, "The Improved Union Churn No. I, Pat. Apr. 27, 1875," 17″ wide, 14″ deep, 31″ high, **$325.**

Highchair with rose design on back rail. 17″ wide, 39″ high. In
Illinois, **$200.**

Dropleaf work or bedside table, maple. 21½″ wide, 18″ deep, 28½″ high; leaves 7¼″. In Indiana, **$225.** Sewing rocker, 35″ high, **$165.**

Pine desk with slant top. 28″ wide, 23½″ deep, 40″ high. In Iowa, **$425.** Hitchcock-type chair, **$125.**

Chimney cupboard in pine. 23″ wide, 13½″ deep, 58½″ high. In Illinois, **$250.** Spice cabinet with porcelain labels, **$115.**

Dark pine corner cupboard. 30″ wide, 18″ deep, 48½″ high; top open shelf painted black can stand or hang. 21″ wide, 10″ deep, 39½″ high. In Illinois, both pieces, **$700.** Pantry boxes, 2″ to 15″ diameter, **$25** to **$75.** Birdcage Windsor rocker, **$450.** Spice cabinet, ash, five drawers, **$500.**

Maple rope bed with some tiger maple, extended to 82″ long, 52″ wide. In Iowa, **$425.** Bedside table, pine, 23½″ wide, 14″ deep, 28″ high, **$165.**

Commode washstand. 29″ wide, 16″ deep, 38″ high. In Illinois, **$245.**
Laundry stove, cast iron, 20″ wide, 17″ deep, 19½″ high. **$125.**
Stenciled butter churn, 10½″ square, 33¼″ high, **$195.**

Slant top Jersey Coffee box, 100 pounds. 21½″ wide, 16¼″ deep, 32″ high. In Illinois, **$275.** Trunk, dated 1870, round top, 21″ wide, 15″ deep, 14″ high, **$125.** Stenciled side chair, **$100.** Stool bench, pine, 14″ wide, 8″ deep, 7½″ high, **$45.**

Corner cupboard with milk base pumpkin paint, pegged construction. 48″ wide, 16″ deep, 83″ high. In Ohio, **$425.** Quilt hanging over cupboard door, **$75.** Wooden ironing board, Amish origin, **$45.**

103

Bride's boxes. 11½″ wide, 19″ deep, 7½″ high. In Illinois, each **$1,050.**

Four-drawer dresser in pine. 38″ wide, 17″ deep, 35″ high. In Iowa, **$375.**

# 6   The parlor is pleasing

How would you like to make your own splint to replace the seat and back in an old rocking chair? That's what one woman did recently. If you want to try it, here are some tips taken from the notes she jotted down as she reviewed her method:

"Cut down a shagbark hickory tree about five or six inches in circumference in May when the sap is coming up. With a draw knife, remove the outer bark. Score from one end to the other however wide you need. Use a linoleum cutter to cut up and down strips. Peel away from top. Roll up strip and let dry, and then boil. Keep each strip in hot water while weaving. Start an end with a carpet tack underneath. Wind over rounds — front to back, again and again. Weave through this foundation over, under. Pattern both sides. Sometimes, it takes two people working together to accomplish certain steps." The picture shows the hickory splint seat and back in the herringbone weave that resulted. That's really getting back to basics.

Splint armchair rocker. 24″ arm to arm, 40″ high. In Iowa, **$165.**

Rocker with heavy rolled arms, some remains of black paint and stenciling. 21½″ arm to arm, 38″ high. In Illinois, **$165.**

Rockers come in all sizes and styles, proportioned for all ages — wee ones, teens, ladies, and men. Often, the rockers were built solidly with the legs in the back extending up through the seat of the chair to the top. The uprights and support posts descended clear through the seat for added strength. The rockers were fastened on the outside of the legs, and the rolled arms were of generous size.

105

When Americans first attached rockers to chairs, they put them on cut-down Windsors. The Boston rocker was the first original style developed. It was named for the Revolutionary War "Tea Party" city because it originated in that area. While they have many spindles in the back as Windsors do, the Boston rockers also resemble fancy chairs because they are painted and decorated with fruits, flowers, and lines. The seats have their own design, which gives individuality. When the back spindles are tapered gently to fit the body's contour, the rocker is indeed comfortable. Many people treasure the worn dark paint and bright flowers. They do not want their Boston rockers bare. They say, "No, don't strip!" The first two pictured on page 105 have kept their old-time finishes. The three on this page have fresh coats of varnish.

Boston rocker, original black and gold trim finish. 41½" high. In Connecticut, **$250.**

Boston rocker, original finish. 38½" high. In Connecticut, **$250.**

Boston rocker, hand-rubbed finish. 42½" high. In Illinois, **$350.**

Boston rocker, hand-rubbed finish. 38″ high. In Illinois, **$175.**

Boston rocker, hand-rubbed finish. 38½″ high. In Illinois, **$250.**

Notice the thinness of the rockers that are inset into the legs on the diminutive rocker (upper right). They may be called "carpet cutters" because of their tendency to rub away at rugs. The bottom edge of the seat is chamfered (beveled), and the legs have a good splay (outward slant).

Sewing or work type rocker. 28″ high. In Illinois, **$165.**

Pine mammy's bench with child's compartment missing. 60″ wide, 17″ deep, 29″ high. In Illinois, **$750.**

For plural seating arrangements, benches were accommodating. The Windsor feel is readily apparent in one with many spindles in the back. Some benches were equipped with rockers. A portion of the seat might have a rail in front so that an infant could be placed behind it. The mother could sit alongside, rock, and perhaps do handwork as she tended the baby.

A Vermont dealer questioned why such benches are referred to as mammy benches. She feels this sounds like a Southern term. According to her, this is a misnomer because mammy benches originated in the North.

108

Rocking bench, pine, slat back. 42″ wide, 17″ deep, 14″ to seat, 29½″ high. In Pennsylvania, **$600.**

Pine settee (often called deacon's bench). 60″ wide, 15″ deep, 32½″ high, **$650.** Quilt on bench, 69½″ by 58″. In Nebraska, **$85.**

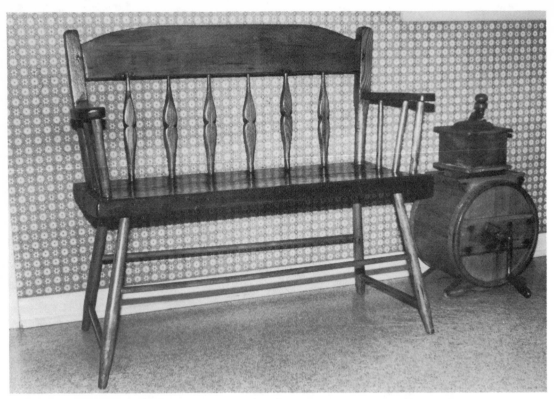

Deacon-type bench. 38″ wide, 14½″ deep, 32″ high. In Iowa, **$550.**

Daybeds were popular in the past century. Frequently, they were referred to as a hired man's bed because that's where the workman slept.

Maple daybed. 72″ wide, 24″ deep, 32½″ high; extends 20″ for extra sleeping space. In Illinois, **$475.**

Could you have lived on eight dollars a month during the years following the Civil War? An Army desk, exhibited by an Indiana dealer, stood at attention at a suburban Chicago mall show. A sign placed on it read "Please don't touch the papers as they are fragile." By hunching and scrunching, it was possible to read some material without fingering it. One pertained to pension provisions for a soldier's widow. She received eight dollars monthly. The two-piece, tabletop desk contained paperwork with various dates. One read, "Dept. of the Interior, Bureau of Pensions, Washington, D.C., June 19, 1893." And another stated, "Quartermaster Notice to Pensioners, Treasury Department 1888."

During the Civil War (1861-1865), desks similar to the one pictured here, were used by the military. This has heightened interest in these desks, made in the years immediately before and after that war.

Fortunately, there were desks used for more peaceful purposes. Among those pictured: An early pine, country desk with a hand planed drawer bottom. The original paint remains on the desk, displayed at a Virginia mall.

Tabletop military desk. 38″ wide, 25½″ deep, 41″ to table top, 69″ overall height. In Indiana, **$850.**

Pine desk. 24½″ wide, 17½″ deep, 27½″ high. In Virginia, **$195.**

Walnut desk with slant top and breadboard ends, replaced pulls. 37½″ wide, 24″ deep, 32½″ high. In Ohio, **$375.**

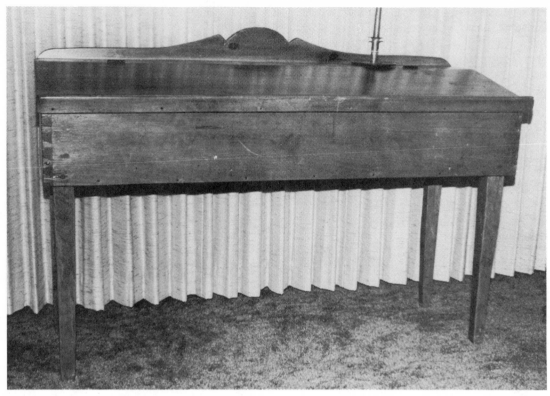

Pine schoolmaster's-type desk with dovetailed ends, lift lid, Pennsylvania circa 1850. 54″ wide, 19½″ deep, 32½″ high. In Illinois, **$650.**

A desk made wide and narrow because that's how a Pennsylvania schoolteacher liked it. It was rustically constructed in the mid-1800s with straight, plain legs that took less skill to make than those that are turned. The legs extend through the bottom of the lift-lid storage section. The heavy, irregular dovetails shout, *Country!*

A desk made by a Wisconsin grandfather because his family needed it. He made the desk between 1900 and 1910 with wainscoting, or up-and-down boards joined by a continuous tongue in one board that locks into a matching groove in another.

Wainscot desk, made in Wisconsin about 1910. 28½″ wide, 19″ deep, 49½″ high. In Illinois, **$375.**

Pine desk; user needed high stool or stood to work. 32″ wide, 27″ deep, 42″ high. In Maryland, **$475.**

Bureau desk with vertical document drawers. 35½″ wide, 16½″ deep, 48″ high. In Illinois, **$800.**

A small, standing-type school desk was complete with student writing slates on top. The stool pictured on page 29 was the type probably used with this desk.

A table from the past that fits in well with today's country furniture theme has legs that curve to a point. This style is uncommon, but not rare, and indicates a French influence. This Ohio stand was made from walnut.

Walnut table stand; legs pegged into apron. 18½″ square, 27½″ high. In Ohio, **$200.**

Work table, maple and poplar. 24″ wide, 20″ deep, 28½″ high. In Illinois, **$125.**

Utility table. 1¼″ thick top, 38″ wide, 21½″ deep, 30½″ high. In Illinois, **$285.**

An unusual feature on another stand is the treatment of the two drawers. One is wider than the other. The contrast of the light and dark woods adds charm.

The parlor of yesteryear was out-of-bounds unless visitors of consequence were being entertained. The casual atmosphere in a home of the present accepts the parlor as an everyday room that is meant to be used for all family activities.

# 7  The bedchamber

**W**hat connection is there between a bedchamber and a tool that resembles an enlarged wooden clothespin? Really, there is a relationship. In the days before the general use of springs on a bed, ropes frequently were interlaced to form a foundation for the mattress. The ropes frequently sagged under the weight they held. The strange, two-prong pins were actually wrenches that managed to pull the ropes taut again.

On rope bedsteads, pegs were spaced equidistant on all four sides of the frame. Ropes were laced around these pegs and strung in parallel lines from head to foot and crosswise to form a webbing on which to set the feather bed (a ticking filled with thousands of feathers). Through the years, changes occurred. Coil springs and firm mattresses replaced the sinking, soft feather bed and the sagging ropes. Chamber changed to room, and bedstead became bed.

Bed wrenches used to tighten ropes on rope beds. Upper left: 14½″ wide, 18″ long. In Connecticut, **$45.** Lower right: 16½″ wide, 13″ long, **$16.**

A top rail that revolves on a rope bed is called a blanket rail. A cover could be placed on it to be rolled off to provide warmth when the house grew chilly during the night. Years ago these authors thought this was a flaw and glued such a rail firmly in place. *We made that mistake only once!* Rope bedsteads retained their popularity throughout most of the 1800s (about 1820-1880).

Maple rope bed. 75½″ long, 54″ wide, 43½″ high. In Wisconsin, **$545.**

Cannonball rope bed, maple. In Connecticut, **$750.**

Cannonball rope bed, maple and poplar. 70″ long, 52½″ wide, 54″ high. In Ohio, **$650.** Trundle bed on rollers can be seen under bed.

Large, round finials that serve as the top turnings on bedposts are called cannonballs. This bed has been lengthened by inserting new rails ordered from a furniture store. The replacement can be made with a minimum of change. The original rails should be kept so that the bedstead will retain its full value.

Some cannonball beds had a trundle (truckle) bed tucked underneath. The trundle was on casters and was hidden away by day and pulled out at night for children to sleep on. The woven coverlet signed "1835 Ohio" on the footboard of the bed with a trundle was made by professionals. Others were done at home. The women who spent hours making them were truly artists. Some designed their own patterns and guarded them jealously to guarantee that they would remain exclusive originals. Most patterns had names, and some had political connotations. Whig Rose and Democrat Rose, for example. Drunkard's Path is descriptive. Similar patterns might have different names in other areas of the country. A young lad's bed would never be covered with one that suggested travel — he might stray from home. Counterpanes with a dark and a light side were "winter" and "summer" types and would be switched seasonally.

An incised fan design often added interest to a cannonball headboard. Pineapple cuts also were used on the posts. At times, pineapple finials topped the bedposts. When bedsteads were high off the floor, the expression "climbing into bed" meant precisely that. Bedsteps might be a part of the chamber equipment, and some pushed in to form a box by day. At night, the two or three little stairs were pulled out. They kept a vigil alongside the bed, especially when they served a dual function, and a lid in a step could be lifted to expose a chamber pot.

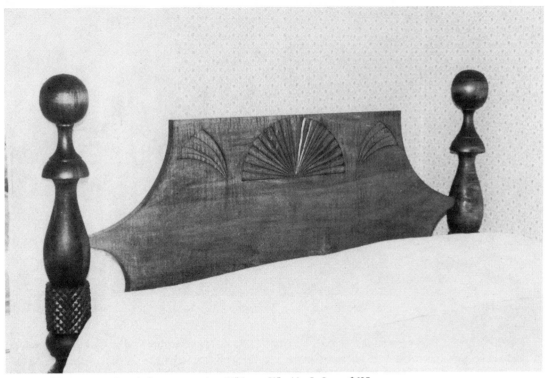

Cannon ball rope bed headboard, three-quarter size. 82″ long, 50″ wide. In Iowa, **$625.**

Other bedroom equipment included washstands and commodes that were discussed in Chapter 3. A primitive table with shelf may have served as a holder for a wash bowl and pitcher. Construction details show hand workmanship. The drawer has a chamfered bottom and fine dovetails. Square nails with the wood darkened slightly around their heads are signs of age. The spiral candlestick on top of the table pictured has an ejector that can be twisted up through the coils so that the last bit of the candle can be burned. This was a practical economy measure. There are wormholes in the off-round, wooden base. Similar holders were used in the late 1700s and continued to be made in the early decades of the 1800s.

Bedside table. 20¼″ wide, 18″ deep, 28½″ high. In Illinois, **$285.** Metal spiral candleholder on top of stand, **$195.**

Cherry blanket chest with dovetailed ends, circa 1840, typical of Pennsylvania. 38″ wide, 17″ deep, 21″ high. In Pennsylvania, **$450.**

Flat top, lift-lid chests were not always confined to the bedchamber, but were also used in the more public rooms. A familial cherry chest is typical of Pennsylvania. A small compartment inside the top edge is called a till, and it held special items such as valuable documents, jewelry, and money.

If the compartment on a lift-lid chest is deep enough to hold blankets, it is called a blanket chest. A drawer at the base provides additional storage space. Wide boards were used in the construction of this chest.

Blanket chest with drawer at base, 35″ wide, 15½″ deep, 30½″ high. In Pennsylvania, **$400.**

118

Trunk, called traveling trunk by family, original green paint, from Maine in 1850. 26½″ wide, 13″ deep, 14″ high. In Pennsylvania, **$295.**

The family calls it a "traveling trunk." When the family's ancestors left Maine in 1850, the trunk shown traveled with them to Pennsylvania. It retains its original green paint.

Butternut is frequently referred to as white walnut. It is light in color and takes a walnut stain well. The chest of drawers pictured dates from about 1840-1860.

Butternut and poplar dresser, double deck on top for storage, circa 1850. It's 40½″ wide, 17½″ deep, 38½″ high. In Ohio, **$425.**

119

A modern housewife requires "lots of closet space" — quite a contrast to most homes of the nineteenth century where pegs were inserted into rails along the walls to hold garments. Wardrobes were freestanding closets, not built-ins. Since they were large, wardrobes were difficult to move. A knock-down construction was used frequently. The molding came off the top, the shelves were removable, the back and sides could be parted, and the base was one unit. The dismantled wardrobe could be transported with ease. Two words of caution, however: *Mark it*. Indicate on underside areas how the wardrobe pieces fit together. You think you'll remember, but you may not after a lapse of time. Slight changes in the wardrobe shown include replacement of the hinges.

The bedroom was a chilly spot in areas where winter storms blew hard and long. People did not linger except for sleeping. In the hot summer before air conditioning, it could be as hot as an oven. Babies were born at home. People generally went to their final sleep in their bedsteads. The bedchamber linked all of life.

Pine wardrobe. 44″ wide, 17½″ deep, 71″ high. In Illinois, **$250.**

Maple cannon ball rope bed. 81″ long, 53″ wide. In Connecticut, **$450.**

Maple bedside or work table. 22″ wide, 17″ deep, 28½″ high. In Illinois, **$185.**

120

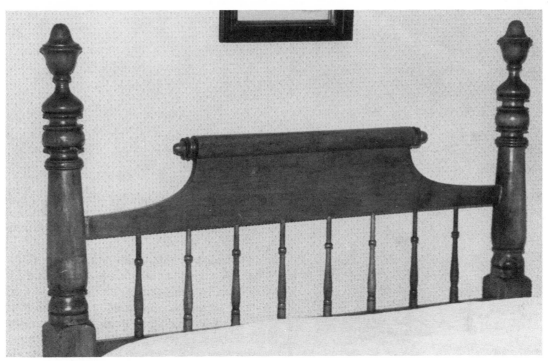

Rope bed with headboard in maple and cherry. 85″ long, 53″ wide. In Iowa, **$550.**

Pine blanket chest, two drawers at base. 50″ wide, 18½″ deep, 39″ high. In Illinois, **$650.**

Pine trunk. 38″ wide, 18″ deep, 18″ high. In Pennsylvania, **$300.**

Pine trunk with dovetailed ends. 28″ wide, 17″ deep, 17″ high. In Wisconsin, **$210.**

Pine trunk with modified dome top. 28″ wide, 16″ deep, 17″ high. In Illinois, **$175.**

Pine trunk with dovetailed ends. 39″ wide, 23″ deep, 25″ high. In Wisconsin, **$295.**

Pine trunk. 28″ wide, 17½″ deep, 22″ high. In Illinois, **$165.**

Pine trunk with slight dome top. 36″ wide, 19½″ deep, 23½″ high. In Connecticut, **$150.**

Pine trunk. 28½″ wide, 19″ deep, 19½″ high. In Illinois, **$145.**

Cherry dresser with two decks. 47″ wide, 21″ deep, 44″ high, 8½″ back rail. In Illinois, **$650.**

Cherry bureau commode. 37″ wide, 18½″ deep, 30¼″ high. In Illinois, **$345.**

# 8  Dab it on!

What an attractive immigrant from Norway! A little trunk inscribed with the words "Caroline, Olaf's Daughter, Bergen." Perhaps, Olaf made the trunk as a gift for Caroline when as a bride, she set sail for America. The iron portions are hand forged and the original key remains in the lock. A till (small compartment at the top) must have held Caroline's most valuable, tiny treasures. People from the Scandinavian countries like vivid, allover designs. Many of their trunks are very colorful creations.

The Pennsylvania Dutch, in contrast, put their paintings in neat panels. They liked hearts, birds, flowers, and angels, and they were really not of Dutch origin. They were Germans. When they arrived in this country, they said they were "Deutsch" — which means "German." Their neighbors thought of Holland, instead, and so these people were dubbed "Pennsylvania Dutch." They painted many chests from the 1700s through the mid-1800s.

Decorated and painted trunk, 1880, brought to America from Norway. 42″ wide, 21″ deep, 20″ high. In Wisconsin, **$865.**

When people wanted furniture that resembled articles made from expensive woods, they took sponges, feathers, brushes, combs, or other utensils and made their own wood grains. The mahogany or rosewood that resulted was skillfully done, and advertisements of the day indicated that factories also produced artificial graining. As time progressed, someone devised a kit to make the process easier. The small washstand pictured is attractive with its fake grain.

In the 1860s and 1870s, a Boston firm advertised cottage chamber furniture. So many pieces were available, and all matching. It would be overpowering to see a tall bed, wardrobe, bureau, chairs, bedside tables, commodes, washstands, and toilets (mirrors) all assembled as a suite in one room. Their paint would have been fresh and deep. The flowers, birds, and pastoral scenes would have been vivid. The New England Furniture Company, based in Grand Rapids, Michigan, offered to match or coordinate the sets with wallpaper, carpet, or drapery fabrics. How many daisies would you have picked from the group shown? If the draperies also were floral, it would seem as if one were sleeping in a flower garden.

Artificially grained washstand with hole in top for basin. 22½″ wide, 14½″ deep, 29″ high. In Maryland, **$175.**

Painted dresser has artificially grained drawer fronts, center of top, and sections on mirror. 39″ wide, 17″ deep, 78″ high. In Illinois, **$475.**

Bed head- and footboards, artifically grained, painted, and decorated. 76½″ long, 57″ wide, 72″ high. In Illinois, **$375.**

Pine bed, originally part of a three-piece cottage set, painted, stenciled, and grained. 56″ wide, 75″ high. In Illinois, three-piece set, **$1,200.**

Pine head- and footboards, originally part of a painted, stenciled, and grained set. 56″ wide, 78″ high. In Illinois, **$375.**

Some people seek the plain pine under all that brightness. This dismays those who feel that a part of America's heritage is being destroyed by removal of the cheerful designs, false graining, and paint. The beds shown have shed their folk art look.

A Cracker Jack of a bed? Honestly! It's handmade of walnut and painted over. It originally was used at a country retreat maintained for Cracker Jack Company executives who wanted to get away from the office back in the 1900s or 1920s. When the executives' refuge was no longer needed, antique dealers were invited to bid on the furnishings of the various rooms.

Cracker Jack bed, circa 1920, used by executives of company. 81″ long, 36″ wide. In Illinois, not priced.

128

Life-top commode, grained and painted. Real drawer has been removed, fake drawer front to the right, carved walnut handles. 29″ wide, 18″ deep, 29½″ high. In Illinois, **$325.**

Cottage style dresser stripped to pine; handles were replaced by artist dealer. 38½″ wide, 17″ deep, 34½″ high. In Illinois, **$250.**

Dresser, cottage style, painted and hand decorated. 38½″ wide, 17½″ deep, 35″ high. In Illinois, **$350.**

# 9   The children's corner

**D**o you realize that children's highchairs used to be sold with or without tables? That's how they were advertised in mail order catalogs of the late 1800s and early 1900s. Initially, they were merely chairs with legs that were long so that a child could join the family at mealtime. No trays were attached. The plank seat on an early handmade chair is well worn. Scribe lines on the legs to guide the workman when he inserted the rungs are visible. The legs splay (slant out) slightly.

Pine highchair, 11½″ arm to arm, 31″ high. In Illinois, **$75.**

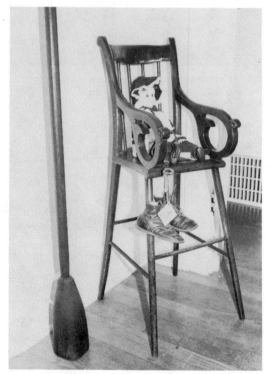

Highchair with rolled arms, 12″ wide, 36″ high. In Ohio, **$165.**

Highchair that converts to stroller. 40″ high. In Illinois, **$210.**

Pine potty chair. 13½″ wide, 11″ deep, 22½″ high. In Illinois, **$85.**

Patented highchairs were popular around the turn of the century. Some had a dual purpose. When pushed down, they became go-carts and served children both at eating and outing.

In the nineteenth century, there was a more delicate and modest term applied to a potty chair. It was called a nursery chair. Today people plop dolls on them or "pot" them with plants. At least that keeps them useful.

Pennsylvania Dutch cradle in cherry. 16½″ wide, 23½″ deep, 42″ high. In Connecticut, **$550.**

Child's armchair (read its tag). 21½″ high. In Illinois, **$50.**

A baby's health was considered when cradles were constructed high at the head to protect the tot from drafts. A Pennsylvania cherry version has cutout heart designs and carved pillars at the head. The slats run lengthwise, and the original paint has been retained. It is probably of Pennsylvania Dutch origin. These people were skillfully industrious and handcrafted many fine items.

Pint-sized chairs were available for children. The one pictured has bentwood arms and a bow back. The original red paint still adheres to it. Black and yellow lines are stenciled on the seat.

Child's rod back Windsor rocker. In Connecticut, **$100.**

Child's cupboard, circa 1800. 10″ wide, 8″ deep, 20″ high. In Illinois, **$300.**

Children also shared in the romance of the Windsor tradition — rod back rockers and chairs were scaled just for them.

It's petite and a treat for a child! The cupboard is a rare salesman's sample, the dealer says. It is handmade with wrought nails, circa 1800. A child would enjoy it because "it's just the size of me!" Pictured at right, above.

What is a salesman's sample? It's a replica of adult possessions fashioned in tiny sizes. Up through the 1860s, it was customary for salesmen to carry samples of their wares to show to prospective buyers. On furniture products, these replicas indicated the construction details, finishes and hardware available, the wood used, and how the item operated. During the 1800s, Grand Rapids, Michigan, was the furniture center of the United States. In 1837, steamboats carried merchandise and passengers. It was not until 1855 when a plank road was built, that overland travel ran smoothly. Horse-drawn vehicles were then able to move in and out of Grand Rapids in all weather.

In 1858, railroads came to the city and helped develop a new merchandising concept. Manufacturers chartered a railroad car, filled it with furniture, and it traveled to all the towns along the tracks accompanied by a salesman who took orders and sold merchandise.

Sometime after 1862, this practice declined sharply. Elias Matter, a Grand Rapids furniture maker, realized that photographic techniques had been greatly improved. He decided to take pictures of his merchandise and print booklets (catalogs) to send with his sales staff. This idea proved so successful that others copied it. Pictures could show the necessary details well, and the manufacture of salesmen's samples became uncommon.

Child's one-piece cupboard. 21″ wide, 11″ deep, 19″ to step, 37″ overall height. In Illinois, **$175.**

Meanwhile, children were not forgotten. Scaled-down versions of adult furniture also were made for playtime. For example, the one-piece cupboard that features an unusual treatment at the base with a type of Dutch door. Glass tops and wooden base portions divide the doors.

Often, a child's pine cupboard styled "just like Mom's" had tongue and grooved doors. Inspection reveals that the bottom door at the left has been replaced by duplicating the original construction. The older one is rougher, shows patina (natural darkening with age), and is a different type of pine (below, left).

Wainscoting is present on the small pine dry sink shown. The top projects over the base.

Child's cabinet, pine. 26″ wide, 13½″ deep, 55″ high. In Illinois, **$525.**

Child's dry sink, pine. 20″ x 20″ top, 26½″ high, 5¼″ splashback. In Iowa, **$395.**

Crossed legs created an unusual desk, especially with a pressed design on both the rolltop and the back rail.

Recently, a group of Cub Scouts studied pioneer days. They ground corn in an obsolete farm grinder, ground coffee beans in an old mill, and rubbed socks on a washboard before putting them through a wringer. The Cub Scouts became aware that washdays of the past were exhausting. In those days, women heated and carried water, bent for long hours scrubbing heavy work garments by hand, and hung clothes outside in any weather. It was hard work. The Cubs enjoyed their brief introduction to washday. They should have had a toy such as this one to test their home art skills.

Child's oak rolltop desk, trestle legs. 22½″ wide, 14½″ deep, 32″ high. In Illinois, **$125.**

Child's toy washtub and wringer, 9″ diameter, 5″ high. In Illinois, **$45.**

Child's pine farm wagon; sides lift out to make coaster wagon, circa 1915. 32″ wide, 16″ deep, 26″ high. In Iowa, **$295.**

Child's wagon, iron spoke wheels, vestiges of green paint remain, circa 1880. 28″ wide, 14″ deep. In Illinois, **$185.**

Riding toys brought joy to girls and boys. "Oh playmate, come out and play with me!" is a delightful sharing chant. Vehicles to ride in or on have always been popular. Wagons were good for many purposes. It was fun for friends to alternate pulling and riding. If a big sister wanted to pull her little brother, high sides kept the toddler from falling out. When two daring buddies got together, they coasted gleefully down bumpy hills. The sides could be removed to make a coaster wagon. A lone lad could push himself about with one leg extending to the ground and the tongue held in his hand to turn the wheels. This version with the wooden spoke wheels is circa 1915.

A slightly older version has metal wheels and a body with the green paint still clinging. It was new in about 1882.

A scooter could move pretty fast with one leg pushing. Downhill glides were bonus times when both feet could be on the board.

A push-pull riding toy is called a handcar in toy catalogs, circa 1915. It required energy to operate one.

Child's scooter. 36″ long, 31″ high. In Illinois, **$35.**

Child's push-pull riding toy. 32″ long, 13″ wide, 11″ high to seat, circa 1915. In Illinois, **$48.**

Some of the stenciling still shows on the pull sleigh pictured. The puller could stand inside the handle if he chose.

Years ago, people used to make toys for tots. Many people do so currently because they enjoy being creative and like to surprise and please a child. The general trend, however, seems to be for adults to latch on to childhood items of yore. Collectors display their dolls and teddy bears using child-size articles. Glass tops were added to wagons for use as coffee tables. Wagons also can haul wood, or store it near fireplaces. Toys from the past are no longer in a child's world. (Have you priced toy farm machines lately? They are expensive.) Children's items do have charm, and "kids" with graying hair enjoy them.

Child's sleigh. 36″ wide, 14″ deep, 48″ to top of handle. In Illinois, **$240.**

Child's low potty chair in hickory and oak with tray. 21″ high. In Illinois, **$145.**

Windsor-type highchair. 13″ arm to arm, 32½″ high. In Pennsylvania, **$165.**

Oak highchair. 42″ high. In Illinois, **135.**

Child's ash and oak cabinet with mirror. 22″ wide, 9½″ deep, 40″ high. In Illinois, **$300.**

Child's pine cupboard. 15″ wide, 8″ deep, 22″ high. In Illinois, **$285.**

Child's cupboard with glass side panels. 26″ wide, 12″ deep, 49½″ high. In Illinois, **$325.**

Pine cradle with one-piece boards on base and sides. In Pennsylvania, **$185.**

Pine cradle. 36½″ wide, 17″ deep, 20″ high. Rockers extend 6″ on each side. In Illinois, **$200.**

Toy cradle, painted green. 29″ long, 10½″ deep, 13½″ high. In Illinois, **$250.**

Two small pine trunks. Below, 19″ wide, 11″ deep, 10½″ high. In Illinois, **$75.** Top trunk, 12″ wide, 7½″ deep, 6½″ high. **$30.**

🌲 🌲 🌲

# 10    Want a peek?

**P**eople are curious. They want to know, "How do others use their country pieces, antiques, and collectibles, in their homes?" To answer this, we'll put on our flying shoes and travel to various sections of the United States.

Ohio porch setting, used as clean-up area, includes zinc sink, porcelain dipper, and kitchen chair.

A young Ohio couple scrimped and searched for years to find an older home in which to raise their little family. They were excited when they found a brick one in town. Like many homes of its day, a massive barn occupies the rear of the lot. Since it was built in the early 1900s, the barn also has a garage section. The former owners were wealthy enough to own a horseless carriage as well as the standard animal-drawn vehicles.

On the wide back porch was a zinc sink for arranging flowers or washing freshly picked vegetables — or kids dirty from play. It was the ancestor of today's mudroom. Evidently, it was an added thought because it is possible to note a hole in the roof and floor of the porch — both carefully patched — where the cistern was added to provide the source for the water. By her choice of accessories that included a washbench, bow back kitchen chair, a communal dipper, and a granite-ware kettle, the young owner established a rustic setting with a practical purpose.

Enter a kitchen in a Chicago area apartment. Refugees from a drugstore soda fountain are the ice cream chairs and table. Since the table required a new top, the young wife enrolled in an adult education class and made one. Wall decorations include a variety of inexpensive kitchen collectibles — a nutmeg grater, a lemon squeezer, tongs, a pancake flipper, and spoons. The two shelves are bread pans from a long-gone bakery. When they were discovered in a small antique shop, they held greasy encrustations accumulated from years of use. A water-rinse paint remover and vigorous rubbing with steel wool removed the built-up grime. A sudsy bath and rinse followed. Holes were made in the top pan, and the unit was hung. A beginner's napkin holder collection is included on the shelves. An Ohio dealer owned similar pans. He cut his apart, decorated them individually for snack trays and priced them at fifteen dollars apiece.

A display in a Connecticut shop shows how a workbench dominates a rustic setting. Notice the harvest or field jug with the brown glaze. Its spout is set at a right angle to the handle. This made it easy to take a swig, and everybody at work in the hot fields used the jug freely. The checkerboard from the early 1800s combines fun with frugality. The flip side has an apple peeler on it.

In the Buckeye State, a vintage water bench with a hole at the right for a wash basin, holds dried flowers and herbs. The small, punched tin cabinet is new, but some of the other items are old in this rustic grouping that says, "My home is not a carbon copy of the others on the street. It reflects my individuality and decorative creativity."

Ice cream table with replaced oak top, three chairs. In Illinois, the set **$245.**

Workbench. 79″ long, 26½″ deep, 32″ high. In Connecticut, **$725.** Field jug on left, circa 1860, **$75.** Wooden bowl, **$75.** Early 1800 checkerboard with apple peeler on reverse side, **$138.**

Water bench. 48″ wide, 16″ deep, 30″ high. In Ohio, **$165.**

Grain shovel. 35″ high. In Connecticut, **$150.** Pine bench, 48″ long, 6″ deep, 11½″ high, **$65.** Farmer's basket, **$30.**

A Connecticut summer home is completely country. Its owner maintains a mall shop in her native New York City. There, her one-piece, wooden grain shovel would be listed at two hundred and fifty dollars, partly because of the high overhead. In her Connecticut shop, however, the price would decrease by about one hundred dollars. Also pictured are a low bench with unique legs that holds a farmer-type basket and a postage stamp quilt.

Trunk. 23″ wide, 12″ deep, 11½″ high. In Connecticut, **$75.** Eighteen-hole candle mold, **$75.** Hanging wall box, **$30.** Stomper, **$12.** Chicken decorated crock, damaged, **$150.**

Frederick Gordon Roe, onetime editor of the *Connoisseur,* suggests in his book *Home Furnishing with Antiques* that it is possible to decorate with damaged articles by turning them so that the bad spot is not apparent. In our setting, the gray crock with the blue chicken pecking on it is imperfect, but it adds to the decor even with one handle (or ear) missing. Helping to provide a unified look are the duck decoy resting atop the crock, the eighteen-hole candle mold, a hanging box with divisions, a stomper, and a small trunk. A country desk from Nantucket Island, just off the Massachusetts coast, and a rush seated chair seem to extend an invitation to their next occupant to share his secrets as he pens a letter, writes a verse, or muses privately.

Desk. 36″ wide, 18″ deep, 39″ high. In Connecticut, **$750.** Rush seat chair, **$125.**

145

Copper bed warmer. 12″ diameter, 42″ long. In Illinois, **$300.**
Blue grass header, 11″ wide, 18″ high, **$55.**

Take note of the pictures of a brick wall with attention-arousing hanging objects on display in a suburban Peoria, Illinois, home. The brass bed warmer with its lidded hot coal container is old, but its handle has been replaced. A bluegrass header, now holding a dried assortment, was a tool that was swung to collect seeds from the grass. It is sometimes confused with a cranberry scoop. On the mantle behind the wood-burning stove sit a wooden duck decoy, a wooden mortar and pestle, several decorated crocks, and an oil lamp. A brass bucket in the foreground holds ashes. The setting is warm, comfortable, and country.

A floor arrangement groups a basket with foliage, a sugar bucket, and a butter churn of the dasher type.

A fireplace setting with brass bucket in foreground. In Illinois, **$95.** On mantel from left to right: oil lamp, **$45.** German beer pitcher (rare), **$375,** wooden mortar and pestle, **$125,** hand-carved wooden duck, **$45,** and peg lamp (satin glass), **$150.**

Oak butter churn. 21″ high with 10″ plunger rod. In Illinois, **$250.**

146

The pine work table pictured was retrieved from a farm home that was about eighty to one hundred years old. When a pioneer era, two-room log cabin was moved to become a part of a new home, the table was discovered in the cabin. It dates to the early 1800s.

A plate rail does not display hand-painted plates but has found a new role in accenting treenware-small wooden objects.

Following World War II, a young married man returned to college to earn a degree. He needed a desk, and his wife wanted this one from an antique shop. They were poor and had no extra cash. At first, they rejected its appealing appearance, but soon it was moved into their apartment when they realized that it was priced lower than a new desk and was of better quality. It's been a member of the household ever since.

Country collectors seem to expose as much in as little space as possible. To them, tasteful clutter, with lots of color, is to be tolerated and shared.

Work table, pine. 29″ wide, 20″ deep, 30″ high. In Illinois, **$225.**

Two-piece drop front desk. 40″ wide, 27½″ deep, 60″ high. In Illinois, **$650.**

# 11 Hang-arounds

**T**he next time you see a wart or hump on a tree, you can call the disease growth by its proper name. This malformation is a burl. Its irregular, pronounced grain produced interesting patterns for decorative touches on furniture such as veneered panels or inlay work.

Walnut burl bowl. 5½″ diameter, 3½″ high. In Illinois, **$85.**

Butter paddles, plates, mortars and pestles, and many bowls were made from the dense burl wood. Naturally, there are fewer examples of objects made from burl wood available so they are sought avidly by specialized collectors.

Small wooden articles represent treenware. It is the word "tree" with an "n" at the end. In addition to the items already listed, spoons, scrapers, dippers, scoops, small hanging boxes, and even spinning articles are treenware. Early examples were fashioned by hand at home. The rough marks left by hand tools are fun to find. These should have softened with age as the pieces were handled, washed, and dried. When you see batches of rustic bowls where the cut lines are overly prominent and crude, entertain a thought that they may have been made recently. A small town craftsman tried to make his wife's kitchen articles as nicely as he could, and age has trimmed off the rough edges. Some, of course, would have been weathered, but isn't a whole stack a little overdone?

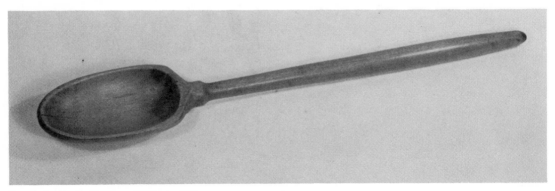

Berry-stained ladle. 13″ long. In Illinois, **$35.**

148

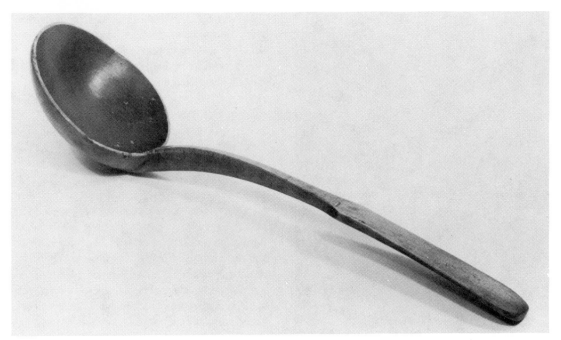

Maple spoon with deep wooden bowl. 16½″ long. In Illinois, **$27.50.**

When products became worn, a frugal family did not toss them out. A favorite bowl developed a split, but retained its usefulness — it was *laced together.* In like fashion, a small section of a worn metal grater could be salvaged by attaching it to a board backing.

Maple mixing or chopping bowl; split end is laced together. In Ohio, **$55.**

Note the shirred Ohio-made rug. Thin strips of shirred or gathered cloth of various lengths were sewn to a heavy backing to create a pattern similar to that of a hooked rug. The owner claims this all-wool example weighs a ton. Recycling is not a new concept. Thrifty housewives got more mileage out of worn garments by salvaging the good portions to cut into narrow strips for rugs. Dye freshened faded fabrics. A hooked rug was fashioned with the aid of a large, thick needle with a hook on the end. Small sections of cloth strands were pulled up through a heavy fabric backing, and a loop was left standing on the top. Other loops of the same height were pulled through to form compact rows. By using different colors, a woman could form flowers, geometric designs, patriotic symbols, or scenes. Her cloth strips were her paints. Her needle was her brush, and she made homey pictures to adorn her floors. Later, printed patterns replaced designs a home-maker had made for herself. People continue to hook rugs, but shirred rugs are hard to find.

New England butter churn; body is one piece of wood. 8″ diameter, 19″ high. In Ohio, **$265.** Yarn winder, 46″ high, **$265.** Kraut cutter on short legs, red paint, 21½″ wide, 8¼″ high, **$145.** Ohio rug, **$75.**

Mirrors experienced a shattering metamor-phosis when they were broken. Glass was so precious on the frontier that the larger broken pieces would be salvaged and inserted into wooden frames that were made to accommodate their strange new shapes. Pioneers saved and "made do" with what they had.

The churn shown is made from one piece of wood. It came from Maine and bears red paint. The long handle is a dasher that is moved up and down to agitate the cream to convert it into butter. The lumps of butter were then molded into desired shapes or stored in stoneware butter crocks. The Ohio yarn winder in the middle wrapped strands of spun wool, cotton, or flax into skeins for weaving or knitting. Behind it stands an Ohio kraut cutter on legs. The double-edged blade that sliced the cabbage as it was held down and pressed back and forth across it can be seen. There is red paint on the frame.

Pantry box with damaged lid. 7½″ diameter, 4½″ high. In Illinois, **$15.**

Lidded storage containers, called pantry boxes, nestled in the pantry, a small room off the kitchen where cooking utensils and ingredients were kept. They ranged in size from tiny ones for pills to those large enough for herbs or cheese. Some of graduating sizes were made to nest one inside the other. Naturally, there were "stuff" boxes for miscellaneous odds and ends. The sides were made of thin sheets of wood that overlapped and were held by nails. Some were round, but many quality pantry boxes made by members of the United States Society of Believers, a religious communal group, were oval. Believers trembled as they worshiped God. Frequently, the women danced in rows, and the men in their segregated lines. Since they shook as they moved, people dubbed them "Shakers." Shaker pantry boxes have long, narrow overlaps affixed with brass nails. The brothers and sisters of the group referred to these laps as "fingers."

Note the unusual construction of the lap on the round grain measure at the right of the picture. The wood is butternut.

Butternut grain measure. 8½″ diameter, 5½″ high. In Iowa, **$45.**

Buttocks basket. In Pennsylvania, **$55.**

Baskets are prominent currently. They squat on floors with dried arrangements in them. They hang on walls and dangle from ceilings. They rest on tables and benches, assured that their presence is known in every room in the house.

One favorite is the buttocks basket, shaped, as the name suggests, like a human derriere. It could serve as a gathering basket when a woman went to the henhouse to collect eggs. Now and then, a farm wife had to shoo or lift a roosting, squawk-

151

Flat back field basket with handle. 19½″ wide, 16″ deep, 13½″ high. In Connecticut, **$85.**

Blue on gray stoneware crock by A. Conrad, Geneva, Pa. In Virginia, **$225.**

ing, fluttering hen off a nest to hunt for hidden eggs in the straw. With her filled basket under her arm, the wife returned to her kitchen.

A half basket was convenient because its flat back permitted it to hang up against the wall, or it could stand on its short legs. There were huge baskets for washday use. Wet clothes were carried to the line to be hung up to dry, and the freshly folded dry garments were carried back into the house in the baskets. All sorts of baskets also were used in the fields and barns. Today, they are used for decorative displays.

It is strange to think that a fragile, hand-painted, porcelain plate could share a kinship with a heavy stoneware crock. Yet, their ancestry is the same. These ceramic products were once lumps of clay. Porcelain is made of fine clay and is white. It is translucent (won't let you see through but lets light through). Stoneware is made from clay with impurities such as iron in it that give it a gray, tan, or slightly reddish color. It is opaque. Hold it up to a light. It does not permit light to pass through nor can it be seen through. Porcelain is fired at a higher temperature than stoneware and, despite its lighter weight, has surprising strength.

A common glaze on stoneware resulted when salt was tossed into the kiln (oven) while the shaped products were being fired at their highest heat. The salt burned, and its vapors left a shiny coating on the surface of the wares. This is called salt glaze. When the salt hit the wares before it vaporized, slight pitting resulted. A brown glaze, seen on stoneware is commonly called Albany or Texas glaze.

Blue is the usual color of decorations on old stoneware. Flowers, leaves, and arrows enhance the Pennsylvania four-gallon crock that was photographed in Maryland.

152

The name "A. P. Donaghho, Parkersburg, W. Va.," is incised (cut) on this jug. The applied handle bears a thumbprint where the clay was pushed firmly to attach it to the vessel's surface.

A twentieth century pine wall shelf often was used to hold objects such as a stoneware butter crock. Missing lids are not too uncommon. They frequently were broken.

A candle sconce usually had metal attached to the rear to protect the wood from searing or burning. A hand-made dovetail on the back makes this an unusual piece.

Stoneware jug by A. P. Donaghho, Parkersburg, W. Va. 11¼" high. In Virginia, **$60.**

Pine wall shelf. 9½" wide, 7" deep, 12" high. In Illinois, **$65.** Blue-and-white butter crock, **$95.**

Wooden candle sconce has metal in back with punched design. 8½" wide, 5½" deep, 18½" high. In Illinois, **$75.**

The hanging container pictured was used as a silverware cleaner box. Some of its black paint is worn off from years of use. Ashes and a wet cloth were employed to remove tarnish from articles made of silver. Flatware (forks, knives, flat objects as opposed to pitchers, glasses, bowls, etc.) was placed upon the wooden surface and it was polished there. A pumice brick was kept in the box portion.

Pa often made a lidded box for Ma because she needed a place to keep salt. He decorated it with incised flowers (cut into the wood) on the sides as well as on the front in a style resembling that used by the Pennsylvania Dutch.

Wall pipe holders are not readily found. The example shown has its own legs to stand on or it can be hung. The shell design crest and base are well done. The radiating burst on the drawer and the general appearance show that someone with an artistic sense created the box.

Silverware cleaning box. 7″ wide, 4½″ deep, 18″ high. In Illinois, **$65.**

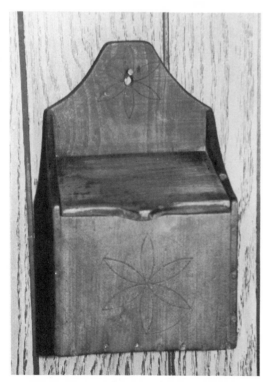

Salt box, with lift lid. 7¼″ wide, 6″ deep, 12″ high. In Illinois, **$55.**

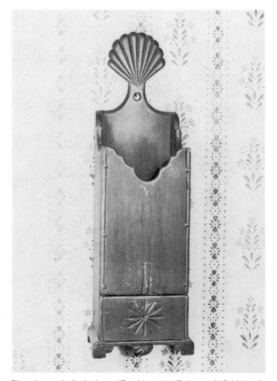

Pipe box, shell design. 6″ wide, 14½″ deep, 20″ high. In Illinois, **$325.**

154

Pine medicine cabinet. 28″ wide, 7″ deep, 23½″ high. In Illinois, **$165.**

Note the double medicine cabinet with small drawers and brass knobs. It has a deep, three-dimensional appearance with oval mirrors set in molded frames. It is pine

A smaller medicine chest was made of cherry and featured a beleveled mirror.

Cherry medicine cabinet. 15¼″ wide, 6″ deep, 28″ high. In Illinois, **$125.**

Pine hanging cabinet. 25″ wide, 9″ deep, 36″ high. In Illinois, **$235.**

A strip of beading is a narrow molding that resembles a string of beads in a continuous line. It's applied at the top of the next cabinet, which also has brass bail handles on two drawers on the bottom.

Panes of glass were small when they were blown by human lung power. It was not until the latter part of the 1800s that flat glass in large sheets was made. Mirror frames were not large in the early 1800s because glass was made in small sizes.

Queen Anne-style pine wall mirror. 15½″ wide, 34½″ high. In Illinois, **$200.**

Hanging mirror, eighteenth century. 14″ wide, 25″ high. In Illinois, **$225.**

It was a German custom to decorate and creatively hand-letter birth, marriage, death, or baptismal certificates that are now called fracturs or frakturs. Angels, hearts, birds, and flowers were executed in watercolors. After the eighteenth century, certificates were printed with blanks left to be filled in with proper names and dates. The picture portion continued to be hand done, and examples may still be found in the Pennsylvania area. The frame with the crisscross corners and applied leaf gained popularity around the mid-1800s.

Benches met a need. They were easier and quicker to construct than chairs. They were for sitting and for the display of objects. The new china doll in the picture helps show that these benches are small. The rear one is pine with bootjack ends. This name was derived from a V-shaped device that gripped the heel securely and helped a person pull off his boots. The red painted bench has bootjack ends and a hand grip in the center of the top. The hog-scraper candlestick served two purposes. At butchering time, its sharp bottom edges removed bristles from a hog. The top held the candle for light at other times. The last bit of candle could be used by moving the ejector lever up in a slot. The beetle bootjack with its V-shaped antennas (feelers) helped remove boots. These are reproduced. Old ones should have wear signs such as paint loss or perhaps some rust, but both of these clues can be simulated. Usually the design, including the back pattern, is more detailed and distinct on the vintage versions.

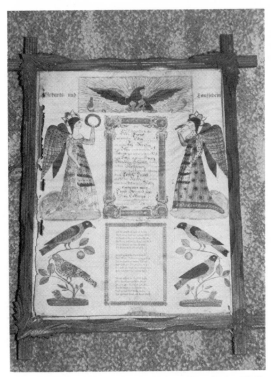

German fraktur, circa 1835, in Victorian walnut frame. 17¼" wide, 21" high. In Pennsylvania, **$110.**

Small bench with bootjack ends. 15" wide, 8½" deep, 8" high. In Illinois, **$22.** Large pine bench. 24" wide, 13" deep, 17¼" high, **$55.** Beetle bootjack. 10½" long, **$40.** Hogscraper candlestick with iron ejector, **$95.** Terra-cotta minstrel, 11" high, **$70.**

157

Pine bench, with small drawer. 18″ wide, 8½″ deep, 11″ high. In Illinois, **$135.**

This little bench pictured has splayed legs. The drawer would be an added advantage as a storage area.

Candle mold in pewter and pine with twenty-four molds, initials "IPM" inscribed. 21″ wide, 6½″ deep, 16″ high. In Illinois, **$1,800.**

People were proud of their possessions. When individuals knew how to read and write (many had no opportunity to learn or lacked the desire), they frequently put their names or initials on objects. "IPM" is inscribed on the pine and pewter candle mold pictured. Pewter, an alloy of tin with lead, brass, or copper, is very soft and melts if it is put over heat. It is unusual to find a mold as large as this. When melted tallow or wax was poured in the cylinders, twenty-four candles could be hardened at one time.

When a lantern is formed from tin with a pierced design punched through the surface, it is referred to as a pierced tin lantern. Such lanterns date prior to 1850.

Tin lantern. 5″ diameter, 18″ high. In Maryland, **$145.**

Vessels were specially outfitted for whaling in the late 1700s and early 1800s. The oil from these huge mammals was used in lamps. A brass whale-oil lamp is pictured. It would be easy to carry because it has a finger grip plus a saucer to catch wax drips.

Dietz lanterns could be purchased through mail order catalogs. The one shown could be carried or hung up. Some Dietz lanterns, circa 1900, were clipped on the front of carriages. When a family arrived home after dark, the mother could remove a lantern and carry it as she herded sleepy children into the house. Meanwhile the father took the other to light his way to the barn where he unharnessed and bedded down the horses. The fuel for these lanterns was kerosene.

Brass whale oil lamp. 6½″ high. In Colorado, **$125.**

Dietz lantern. In Virginia, **$110.**

Imprint on Dietz lantern.

A feature of the next lantern is its high handle that kept a person's hand well above the heat of the flame.

A copper coffeepot of generous proportions has a chain to keep the lid from being lost. The handle on top and the one near the base assisted in toting and tilting.

A trivet was a small metal stand that held cooking vessels near a fire to keep their contents hot. This English brass version is a sliding grate trivet that hooked onto a grate. It moved so that the distance from the heat source could be adjusted. In the strict definition of the term, trivets must have three legs, and they are fireplace equipment. Purists like to call the tri-legged objects upon which sadirons rest, "stands."

Treen items, hanging wall boxes and cabinets, baskets, stoneware, lighting devices, brass and copper implements, and frames are being salvaged from the past to serve as accessories in modern homes. This bridges the generation gap, and helps people to appreciate their heritage.

Brass handled lantern. 3½" square, 9" high to dome top. In Colorado, **$125.**

Copper coffeepot. 9½" diameter at base, 14½" high. In Connecticut, **$125.**

Sliding grate trivet. 20½" long, 5½" wide, 8" high. In Connecticut, **$225.**

# 12    Great grandpa on the job

An 1840 cobbler's bench was never meant to be a coffee table, but that's what it's turned out to be. A youthful model perches where the shoemaker once sat and fashioned shoes. A cobbler was frequently a transient laborer who went from one farm to another to repair and make the families' supply of boots and shoes. He remained as a guest in each home until his work was completed. The leather he needed was usually provided by the farmer from the tanned hides of animals that had been butchered for the winter meat supply.

Pine cobbler's bench with the original work tools and pegs, circa 1840. 48½″ long, 24″ wide at drawer end, 17″ wide at seat end with leather cover. In Illinois, **$475.**

The cobbler prepared all his material before he set to work. He sliced and cut small wooden pegs that were more square than round. He measured feet and cut out the necessary leather. He waxed his thread so that it would slide through the holes he had punched with his awl. He laid out the nails he would need. The cobbler worked hard all day long. At mealtimes, he entertained the family with news from other areas he had visited. His coming was an event eagerly anticipated by isolated farm families. When his tasks were completed, he moved on to his next assignment.

The first example shown includes the tools that performed various tasks in working with leather — piercing, holding, filing, cutting, sewing, and pounding. Small pegs and roughly made nails caught in the cracks and crevices have been preserved.

Pine cobbler's bench with thick plank seat end. 53″ long, 18¼″ wide at compartment end, 14″ high. In Illinois, **$375.**

Pine cobbler's bench; leather missing over hole where cobbler sat. 46″ long, 19″ wide, 12½″ high. In Illinois, **$350.**

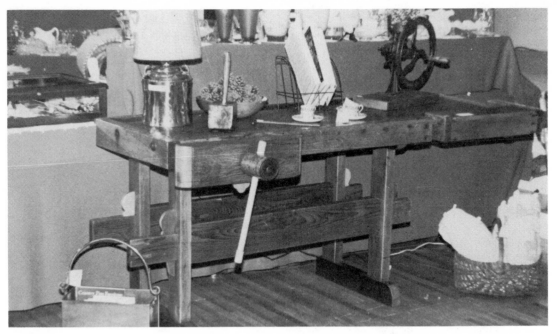

Cabinetmaker's workbench in pine and maple with two vises. 74″ long, 24½″ wide. In Nebraska, **$895.** Corn grinder, **$85.** Wooden mallet, **$24.**

The pine and maple cabinetmaker's workbench pictured now decorates an office. A vise at the front twists tightly to hold items steady. There are tool slots handily available.

Carpenters had specialized chests in which they organized their tools. Chests were put on a wagon to be transported to a work site. Inside the chests were stationary slots and movable compartments that slid out so that various tools, nails, screws, and other necessary items were accessible.

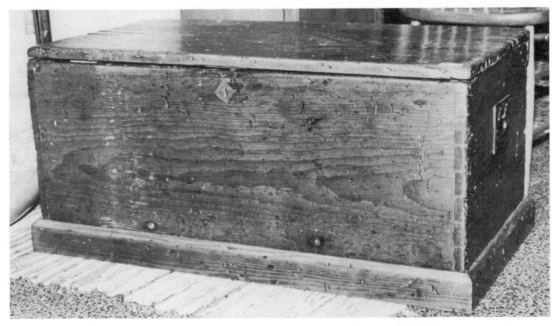

Carpenter's chest with one-piece top, molded base. 36″ wide, 18″ deep, 17″ high. In Wisconsin, **$195.**

Pine carpenter's chest with brass corners and side pieces. 34½″ wide, 19″ deep, 18½″ high. In Illinois, **$165.**

Walnut and cherry carpenter's chest; inset panels on sides and ends, raised panels on top. 37″ wide, 19″ deep, 20″ high. In Illinois, **$275.**

Pine water bottle box, patented May 28, 1893, with handholds for carrying. 14″ wide, 13″ deep, 22½″ high. In Iowa, **$125**.

A farrier was and is a blacksmith, a man who shoes horses. In earlier times he also made and repaired iron objects by hammering them by hand on an anvil (an iron or steel block). First, he heated the iron red hot in a furnace called a forge that was kept running by huge hand-operated bellows. This device blew the coals with a stream of air that passed through a narrow tube when the sides of the bellows were pressed together. The U-shaped metal "shoes" the smithy nailed to the horses' hooves protected their feet. The hinges, latches, andirons, farm and household tools and utensils produced by the blacksmith were essentials in the households of yore. Malleable (can be hammered to shape) iron was made from high quality pig iron that required long heating at high temperatures and slow cooling to make it strong. It was shipped in bars called "pigs." Someone thought that the small sand molds that were placed around a central channel resembled a litter of suckling pigs clustered around the mother. The channel was the nursing sow.

Where should a rocking bottle go? Who knows? Maybe, it was used on construction sites so workers could get cool drinks of water. It was patented and will tilt so that the beverage pours without the need to lift it or remove the bottle from its wooden insulation.

Close-up of imprinted label on water bottle box.

Farrier's tool tote in pine. 21½″ wide, 9½″ deep, 21½″ high. In Illinois, **$95.**

The carrier pictured is a farrier's tool tote. A file for the hooves of the horse to be shoed was placed in the slot. The huge wood and leather bellows that bring back memories of the blacksmith's heyday are sometimes sliced apart to form several coffee tables.

Back in the time when the barber shop was a man's social center, certain furnishings were expected. Generally, each man who came to be shaved had his own shaving mug stored for him in a rack. Partitions separated the individual cups that might have the customer's name or initials on it. The design on some cups depicted its owner's job. Since they were often given as gifts, mugs often had the words "husband," "father," or "brother" in the painted designs. The common mug cabinets are considered primitive items today, although barber shops with elite clientele provided ornate assigned spaces for mugs. Patrons chatted as they waited their turns — and who hasn't heard of barbershop quartets? In many shops, it was possible to pay for the use of a tub. Hot and cold water was carried in to fill it so a man could have a sit-down bath.

The shaving mug rack pictured has incised (cut-in) outlines of shaving brushes and razors on the sides.

Mug rack with scalloped shelf edges, incised designs of shaving brushes and razors on end panels. 29½″ wide, 9″ deep, 41″ high. In Illinois, **$450.**

167

Pine barber's cabinet. 29½" wide, 6" deep, 35" high. In Illinois, **$350.**

A barber's cabinet held the necessary tools of his trade. The shaving brush with its hand-fitting handle had long, soft bristles. It was circular in shape, and its bristles were swished in water and swirled on a bar of soap in the mug to lather the face. A long-handled straightedged razor was slapped up and down on a leather strop for sharpening. The barber needed a steady hand to prevent nicks while removing the beard stubble. Towels swathed the customer to avoid wetting his collar and to stop stray hair from going down his back. Sometimes, the barber used a brush to swish about after a haircut to remove any bits of hair. If requested, pomade was used to slick down the hair and it left a pleasant smell. The barber was skilled at his trade.

Since trains do not chug and whistle along tracks hauling as many riders and as much freight as they once did, people are nostalgic about them. Railroad items are collectible. They bring back memories of times when families packed lunches and climbed aboard for a thrilling train ride to visit relatives or to shop in the big city. The conductor knew how to move with the swaying train as it clacked over the rails. His system of collecting tickets and calling out the names of approaching towns or cities assured all that they would arrive at the correct destination. Included is a picture of a railroad desk that a station agent found handy.

Oak rolltop railroad desk with pull-out work shelf. 30" wide, 26" deep, 49" high. In Illinois, **$850.**

"This is the way we go to church so early on Sunday mornings" was part of a simple singing game that acted out activities associated with each day of the week. Many families came to America in search of a place where they could worship God as they pleased. A candle box from a church sanctuary and two pews are examples of ecclesiastical furnishings that are finding their way into home decors.

And, these reminders of the church past are a fitting close to a look-back at the various occupations that found comfort in a day of rest.

Church candle box with slanting lift lid. 16½″ wide, 11″ deep, 24″ high. In Illinois, **$150.**

Church pew. 64½″ wide, 20″ deep, 29″ high. In Illinois, **$155.**

Pine church pew. 57″ wide, 18″ deep, 30″ high. In Illinois, **$130.**

# 13  Rustic — a best seller

An Illinois couple in a rural area town where many retired farmers live enjoys taking the country to the city. They find anything rustic sells. "People from Chicago go crazy over farm stuff," they exclaimed. "We took a load up to a three-day show and had to leave after the first day. We were cleaned out completely."

What are sophisticated Chicago residents seeking? Country collectibles! It's BIG currently, and here are some typical farm items in demand.

Did you ever hear of the humble little wagon seat that went to church? A Connecticut dealer enjoys one in her home. Now, hear the story of the short, lightweight "bench" that fitted into a wagon — and was removable. First, the parishioners sat on the seat as they rode to their house of worship. At their destination, there might be a mounting block outside the church. The mother and her daughters in their long, full skirts could exit with grace onto this permanent step and then descend to the ground. Father and the boys were detained since they took the horses to the rear of the churchyard to unhitch them. Sometimes, they put them in protective stalls if they were available. Perhaps, the animals required a little food or water or a rubdown after their journey. When the horses were cared for, the males entered the church.

If the church were crowded, a family carried in the wagon seat to sit upon as they worshiped God. It must not have been a comfortable perch. It was so low that legs would have to be tucked in.

Portable wagon seat in pine and maple, could be used where needed. 34½″ wide, 18″ deep, 29½″ high. In Connecticut, **$300.**

171

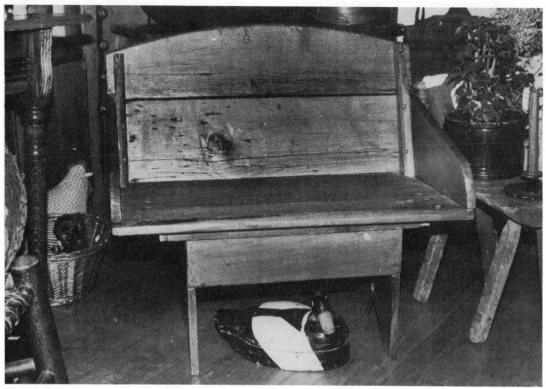

Pine wagon seat sitting on a bench. 28″ wide, 14″ deep, 14″ high. In Illinois, **$125.**

Wagon seat, pine with lift lid. 19″ wide, 14″ deep, 24″ high. In Illinois, **$175.**

Often, the wagon seat and the bench beneath were separate units. Or, a storage unit similar to that pictured was a part of the wagon seat.

Low milk stools were something a farmer could put together quickly out of a piece of log. Stout sticks pushed up through holes to form legs. Three-legged ones were common. The cows had names. Bessie, Elsie, Molly, for example. All the cows were fussy. Each always had to be milked from the same side, at the same time, in the same stall. The farmer drew his short stool close to her flank as his hand repeated a rhythmic squeeze-pull, tugging at the udders to keep streams of milk squirting into the milk pail. A hopeful cat might meow nearby and sometimes caught a stream of

Milk stool. 15″ wide, 8″ deep, 13″ high. In Illinois, **$45.**

Milk stool, 11″ wide, 8″ deep, 11½″ high. In Illinois, **$45.**

the warm goodness aimed at her mouth by the farmer. Milking required a certain knack. In summer, Bessie's tail flipped dangerously close as she slapped away flies. If she were quick tempered and didn't like a yank, she was prone to kick. A farmer might have to duck off his stool quickly, so that a milk pail would not be knocked over and spill its warm, foaming contents.

The housewife received the milk to separate. After the cream rose to the top, she removed it. Much of this thick richness would be churned into butter. Various examples of churns follow. Some are large and may have been used in small dairies. The first picture shows the paddle portion that sloshed the cream about.

Paddle from butter churn. In Illinois, **$35.**

Butter churn with wooden staves and iron bands — dasher type. 33″ high. In Illinois, **$215.**

Butter churn with inside paddle turned by crank. 15½″ wide, 12½″ deep, 16¼″ high. In Pennsylvania, **$165.**

Two-speed butter churn with removable handle. 18″ wide, 12″ deep, 32″ high. In Indiana, **$225.**

Butter churn with paddles in dome head. 32″ wide, 15″ deep, 39″ high. In Maine, **$225.**

174

If you look closely at the photograph, you can see the cow outlined on the churn.

Butter churn, counter or tabletop-type. 13″ diameter, 9½″ deep. In Illinois, **$95.**

Cow design imprinted on back of tabletop butter churn.

Three-legged butter churn was patented Dec. 20, 1864. 20″ wide, 14″ deep, 31″ high. In Illinois, **$225.**

Partly obliterated imprinting on butter churn states that premiums were taken for its design in Ohio, Indiana, Michigan, Illinois, Wisconsin, and New York. Backside of Union Churn, No. 2.

The manufacturer of the pine churn with its splayed legs was proud of his product. The stenciled printing on it reads, "Improved Original Union Churn, Pat. Dec. 20, 1864. First premium taken at the state fairs of Ohio, Ind., Mich., Ill., Wis., and New York." The manufacturer realized he had a quality product.

Butter worker, wooden roller, patented "Mar. 23, 1875," has hole in top to release moisture. 28″ wide, 16″ deep, 17″ high. In Illinois, **$175.**

A butter worker that originally had no legs and sat on a table could possibly have been used for commercial work. It was patented "Mar. 23, 1875." The roller operates when the handle is turned, and a hole permits accumulated liquid to escape.

Next is a cheese maker on which some of the original stenciling is still visible. Replica catalogs from mail order houses of the late 1800s and early 1900s help identify many passé objects that once had a purpose now bypassed by progress. Even if you don't seek to learn about some object from looking through catalogs, they're fun to flip through and are a teaching aid about life years ago.

Cheesemaker in pine has one end higher than other to allow drainage. 40″ wide, 19″ deep, 31½″ high. In Illinois, **$175.**

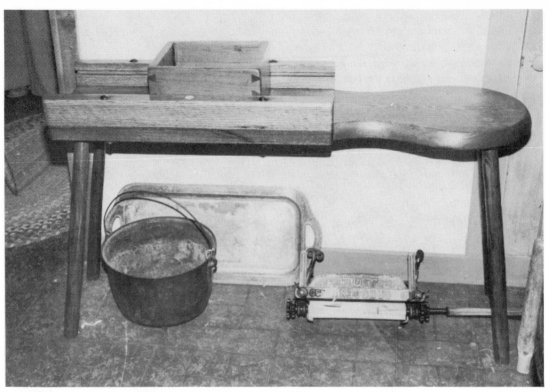

Oak kraut cutter stand. 44″ wide, 12″ deep, 26½″ high. In Illinois, **$275.**

Kraut cutter stand. 37″ wide, 12″ deep, 24″ high. In Illinois, **$227.**

The storybook Peter Rabbit who almost got caught raiding a cabbage patch couldn't possibly eat all the huge crisp heads in a farmer's wife's garden. Much of the cabbage she picked was washed, cored, and placed in the box on top of a kraut cutter. The worker would hold the cabbage down firmly as the box moved back and forth across the blades. Thin strips of cabbage came out to be caught in a bowl beneath the stand. The chopped cabbage was placed in large crocks with heaps of salt and was allowed to ferment in its own juice. The sauerkraut that resulted from this briny treatment was warmed with meat to help feed the family in winter. Two cabbage slicers are pictured at left.

Treenware (small objects made of wood) for the kitchen included a bowl, butter paddle, and scraper. At times when food was sold in bulk form at the grocery store, the clerk might slap off some butter with a paddle, weigh it, and wrap up a pound for a customer.

Round bowl, 12″ diameter. In Illinois, **$45.** Butter paddle, 10¼″ long, **$15.** Scraper, 12″ long, **$12.**

Butter molds. In Illinois, each **$65.**

If a housewife wanted her freshly churned butter to look attractive, she put it in a mold so that the design would be transferred to the top of the pound. Various shapes and sizes of molds, including wee ones for children, were available, but the half-pound size is difficult to find.

Bantam incubator made in Springfield, Ohio. 24″ wide, 16″ deep, 12¼″ high. In Illinois, **$125.**

Chicken coop with added legs and glass top. 35″ wide, 23¼″ deep, 18½″ high. In Wisconsin, **$195.**

Traditionally, if a housewife sold her excess butter and eggs, the money was hers. She might keep the change in a sugar bowl in her cupboard. Some eggs were put into an incubator to hatch, and later it kept the newly hatched baby chicks warm and dry. The Bantam Incubator pictured on the left has the original 1920 labels. A paper label on one side states, "This is Our Cheap Incubator. If you want the best Get the Buckeye Hatcher." A painted, stenciled label on the side says, "Manufactured by the Buckeye Incorporated Co., Springfield, Ohio."

A new supply of chickens was necessary because live, plump hens were sent to market in large coops. Such a crate — with a glass top and feet added — is now used as a rustic plant stand or coffee table.

Seed potato cutter made in Jackson, Michigan. 22″ wide, 13½″ deep, 33″ high. In Illinois, **$145.**

Each year farmers saved some of their best potatoes for seed. Potatoes have small indentations called eyes from which fragile, yellowish-green sprouts grow in the spring. A potato was cut so that a piece with several eyes could be planted in a hole and the ground hilled over it. Usually, there were a couple of pieces to a hill. These would sprout into bushy plants. Only by using these bits of potato could the farmer be assured that the same type would reproduce. The roots formed tubers. If these were dug up in the summer, a small, thin-skinned "new potato" was harvested. When the potato was dug in the fall, larger ones had developed. After the dirt was cleaned off, the potatoes would be stored in a cool dry place for later marketing or eating.

A cutter for seed potatoes that's shown is marked, "Potato Cutter Aspinwall Patents Aspinwall Mfg. Co., Jackson, Mich."

Perhaps, a patented tomato juicer wasn't practical because it shows little evidence of use. It is inscribed, "Pat. 2126045 Parkway 39, Rochester, N.Y. USA."

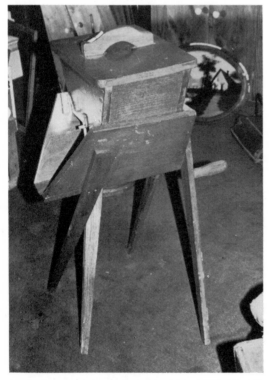

Tomato juicer made in Rochester, New York. 16½″ wide, 11″ deep, 33″ high. In Pennsylvania, **$70.**

Corn sheller attached to side of box with bail handle for carrying. 18″ square, 17″ high. In Illinois, **$115.**

Close-up view of corn sheller.

A corn sheller that was hammered together with old square nails has a swinging handle so it could be transported easily. It was used to grind hardened, dried shelled corn.

An operable harness bench or harness horse that's pictured can be used to make leather harnesses, and it is not a common find. Most have vital parts missing.

Harness bench, complete. 25″ wide, 26″ high. In Illinois, **$145.**

Pine box for picking strawberries. 18″ wide, 13″ deep, 11½″ high. In Illinois, **$35.**

A wooden berry picking basket has a handhold at the top for carrying. The thin wooden quart baskets are collectible now that they have been replaced by cardboard or plastic types.

Coopers fashioned buckets with staves. Metal rings held the wood in place. An early cooper in this country was John Alden who was hired to voyage with the Pilgrims to America aboard the *Mayflower* in 1620. He chose to stay in the Plymouth Colony and "maryed" a Pilgrim lass, "Priscila Mullines." The spellings within the quotations are those of William Bradford, the colony's second governor, who wrote a history of Plymouth.

Have you ever seen a green deer? It's on a weather vane made of copper. Verdigris is a greenish coating that forms on brass, bronze, or copper, and is similar to rust on iron or tin. The coating on this deer appears blotchy. Weather vanes twisted and turned as winds battered them. The vanes indicated the direction of the wind. A favorite sport enjoyed by mischievous boys was shooting weather vanes on top of barns. This vane's deer has been pelted frequently and appears to be seeking escape. Hand-fashioned weather vanes are now considered examples of folk art, and may be seen adorning the walls of homes with even the most modern decor.

Farm articles of yore score with modern families. The rustic appearance adds a sought-for casual look to homes á la country.

Bucket made of pine. 14″ diameter, 6″ high. In Ohio, **$65.**

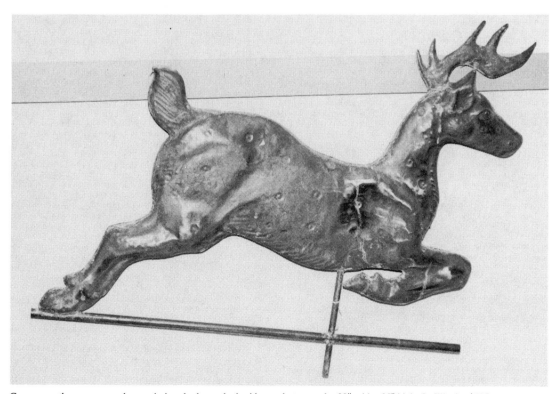

Copper weather vane, one horn missing; body marked with gunshot wounds. 28″ wide, 25″ high. In Illinois, **$195.**

# 14  It's store-bought

**A**miniature department store — that's what a country store was back in great grandpa's day. Not only were groceries dispensed in bulk from barrels, bins, jars, and crocks, but bolts of dress goods and sewing materials were displayed and sold. There also were store-bought clothes (ready-mades), boots, and lamps for sale. There was a mixture of merchandise — and no shopping carts for self-service. The merchant waited on his customers and wrapped their purchases in paper that was torn from racks and then twisted about with string that twirled from holders hung up high. Merchandise was not pre-packaged. It had to be weighed or counted out. If you wanted one large pickle, it was snared for you from a barrel.

Manufacturers eager to promote their products provided merchandising items to display their wares to advantage. Makers of thread put out a wide assortment of spool cabinets in woods such as walnut, oak and, occasionally, cherry. Decorative lettering promoted its competitive contents. Clark praised ONT (Our New Thread). Merrick's suggested its spool cotton was the best.

Spool cabinet with two doors, two drawers. 21″ wide, 11½″ deep, 26″ high. In Illinois, **$250.**

Meal or store bin in pine. 39″ wide, 20″ deep, 24″ to slant top bin covers, 35″ overall height. In Illinois, **$350.**

Such cases now function as ladies' jewelry boxes, are used as coffee tables, or those with desks perform their original duties.

Sectioned bins of various types were essential. Some were large and held provisions such as cornmeal or wheat or rye flour. Many reposed on the floor, and some hung on walls.

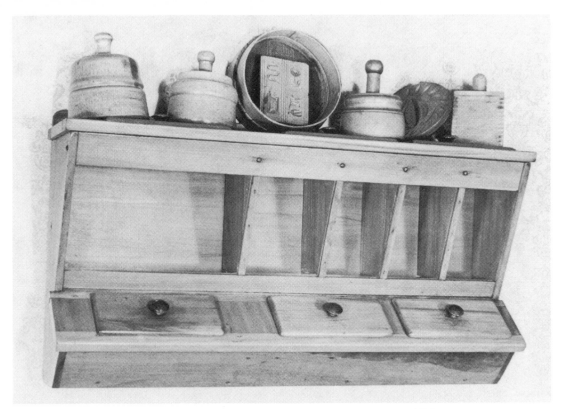

Glass fronted hanging display case. Top lifts. 28½″ wide, 7″ deep at top, 15″ high. In Illinois, **$425.**

Coffee beans were scooped from large, lift-lid wooden bins. The supplier's company name was on the front.

Coffee bin, reads "Roasted Coffee" on lid. 15″ wide, 15″ deep 23½″ high. In Iowa, **$155.**

Coffee bin, some pine replaced. 18″ wide, 14″ deep, 27″ high. In Illinois, **$95.**

Rolltop coffee bin, reads "Combination Coffee." 23″ wide, 17″ deep, 33″ high. In Illinois, **$185.**

Coffee mill, red base, black wheel, gold letters. 27½″ diameter, 15″ wide, 68″ high. In Illinois, not priced.

A large red coffee grinder with a double wheel ground the beans for customers to use in their coffeepots. An unusual variation of the bin combined it with a rolltop desk. Coffee merchants really sought to get the attention of the consumers through their display units.

Plain counter desks were prevalent as each merchant took care of his own accounts. Pine was the usual wood on these small lift-tops with their compartmented insides.

Pine coffee bin. 25″ wide, 17″ deep, 32½″ high. In Illinois, **$165.**

Pine counter desk with lift lid. 15½″ wide, 22″ deep, 9″ high at back. In Illinois, **$95.**

Hardware stores (or a section in the general store) also had specialized display furnishings. Objects such as bolts and screws were kept in multidrawered, rotating octagonal holders. Each size or kind had its own drawer space. The stencils have been preserved on the model shown and indicate the contents on each of the eighty drawers.

Another cabinet has drawers with combination brass pull-label holders into which labels were inserted behind glass to specify the contents.

The brass mortar and pestle illustrated could have been used to crush and mix medicinal potions in a drug store. Apothecary chests were another furnishing.

Butcher blocks are big — in size, weight, and the desire of many people to own them. Several men must stuggle to lift one of these large butcher blocks. Since they are thick sections of wood on legs, they are not easy to move. A home

Hardware store bolt holder with eighty drawers. 21″ wide, 36″ high. In Iowa, **$1,250.**

Oak store cabinet with bottom piece added has glass on drawer pulls for labels. 65½″ wide, 14″ deep, 36″ high. In Illinois, **$375.**

Brass mortar and pestle. Mortar, 4½″ high; pestle 7½″ high. In Connecticut, **$95.**

Pine apothecary chest. 31″ wide, 11½″ deep, 39″ high. In Illinois, **$550.**

Butcher block with galvanized extensions on feet. 39½″ diameter, 30″ high, 6″ thick. In Illinois, **$475.**

Post office box in pine. 38″ wide, 75″ high. In Illinois, **$325.**

economics major maintains they are handy in a kitchen, providing a surface for cutting meats, chopping vegetables, making sandwiches, rolling out pastry, or kneading dough. She calls hers indispensable. Chopping blocks must be kept clean and sanitary. Sterilizing them is recommended.

A good butcher's helper was displayed at an antiques show. It resembled an enlarged shaving brush. However, it had enlongated bristles of metal. It was used by the butcher after he finished scraping up bits of meat, grease, and fat on the block's surface with a knife held firmly by both hands. The metal brush finished the cleaning process. No one wants old fat and grease or wood slivers in food. Blocks often acquire sway tops after years of rough treatment. Some say this adds to their personality.

In a community where the population was not large enough for home delivery of mail, a part of the general store might house a post office. Residents came there to collect their mail, which had been placed in their specific box.

These are samples of store items that are serving humanity again, but in a totally different role. Their use might startle, alarm, or cause their original owners to chuckle gleefully, "Who'd want that old thing in a parlor?" The new owners might shout, "We do! It's rare!" *Country-itis* has claimed them totally.

# 15  Spinning dreams

**B**ack in the early days of this country, women created cloth of cotton, wool, or flax so that they could dress their families. They used spinning wheels to make threads by twisting together plant or animal fibers to give them strength and make them cling together. The process was tedious because only one thread could be spun at a time. Especially fine thread demanded two spinnings.

Next, the yarn was wound off the spindle into hanks on a wooden, hand-held cross-reel called a niddy noddy. This helped prevent kinks, set the twist, and measured the yarn.

A man whittled the tools his wife used out of native woods, usually pine or maple. A niddy noddy had to be measured precisely so that it had a winding circumference of two yards. Much as little girls jumping rope have their counting chants to indicate how well they perform, so the housewife sang niddy noddy songs to help her remember the number of twists she had completed as she wound her yarn into a skein. Forty times equaled a knot, and seven knots produced a skein.

Finally, progress replaced the niddy noddy with a standing reel that could be cranked. Some came complete with a clock device that counted the number of revolutions necessary to make a skein, and the niddy noddy songs became obsolete and forgotten.

Professional dyers were available who would dip the skeins, but usually Colonial housewives achieved beautiful, bright dyes by using indigenous materials. They went out and picked their own colors. Bittersweet produced orange; onion skins yielded yellow; black came from alder bark; goldenrod blossoms made green; and red tones could be achieved from pokeberry, sumac, blood-root, or dogwood. Rich blue dye came from indigo that was imported or grown domestically, especially in the South. Peddlers carried it to remote farm sections.

The spinning wheel pictured was hand fashioned. It is pegged together, and the legs go through to the top. A pedal is missing, but if it were replaced, the wheel could be operated.

Spinning wheel has pegged legs which extend through top; missing pedal. 32″ wide, 10″ and 13″ deep at ends, 40″ high. In Illinois, **$400.**

Spinning wheel in maple and pine. 37″ high. In Ohio, **$375.**

Combination yarn winder and kraut stomper made of tree twig verticals. 26½″ diameter base, 35″ high. In Pennsylvania, **$65.**

The second wheel was found in Ohio. Commonly, these small ones were for flax. They were sometimes called Saxon wheels. Flax was a tough fiber, and the worker sat to spin, working it with her hands and her foot. The large spinning wheels were hand operated, and the woman "walked" back and forth many miles each day as she twisted the fibers together to make thread. After this task was completed, it would be necessary to weave the threads into cloth. It was not easy to clothe a family because the woman would still have to cut out and sew the fabrics into garments.

The man who made the yarn winder that's shown took what he had on hand. He grabbed his wife's handmade kraut stomper, added a few boards and some twigs, and his task was done. The result is a true primitive.

Contrast that rustic with the turned arms of the second example. The shop owner calls her manikin "Lady Myrtle May" — she's certainly too well dressed to be concerned with domestic tasks, even if her clothing were from the appropriate period.

Myrtle May the manikin stands guard over yarn winder. 30″ wide, 44″ high. In West Virginia, **$135.**

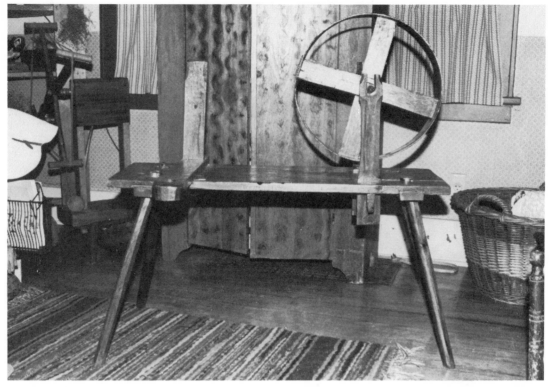

Yarn winder with bentwood wheel. 36″ wide, 11½″ deep, 38″ high. In Illinois, **$155.**

This wheel is of bentwood. The splayed legs go through the top and have wedges driven in them to make them separate to hold tightly. It is an unusual winder.

A yarn winder made of maple, pine, and bird's-eye maple has a counter with a bell attachment.

Yarn winder in pine, maple, and bird's-eye maple, with counter bell for revolution, one arm missing from crosspiece. 16″ deep, 40″ high. In Illinois, **$160.**

Yarn winder. 16″ deep, 42″ high. In Illinois, **$145.**

Sampler has lowercase letters in black, capital letters in red. 13½″ wide, 18½″ high. In Illinois, **$75.**

A winder with four arms also is shown. And, some with eight have been known to function. The skill of the maker helped determine how fancy the yarn winder would be.

There is renewed interest in fabrics today, and a return to hand crafts. People are acquiring old spinning wheels or buying new ones so that they can spin their own threads and weave their own cloth. It is interesting to realize that the old, rough, loosely woven homespun cloth was twenty-seven to thirty-one inches in width. Machined imitations are fifty to sixty inches wide.

Samplers have an interesting derivation. Adults used to take a strip of cloth of the desired shape or size and carefully fill it with embroidery or lace patterns that they wished to preserve. Thus, early samplers were a needlework record. Sometime during the 1500s, it became the fashion for young girls to create samplers to practice various stitches as they learned to sew. It was also a way for the skillful to display their ability. Some are simple — the ABC's, numerals, a Bible verse, or a motto worked with colored silks stitched on linen or wool backgrounds. Others are elaborate with human figures, birds, flowers, and intricate designs blended to produce an artistic result. At times, the name of the seamstress, her age, and the date are included.

Every female child was supposed to be able to sew a variety of fancy stitches. The customary age to start learning this art was four. After all, a mid-teen bride was expected to have about a dozen of her own-made quilts to include in her dowry.

As a general rule, samplers dating back to the 1700s were usually longer than wide. Next, square ones became popular. As 1900 neared, the art was fading away, and low, wide backgrounds were utilized. The shape, therefore, is a rough guide to sampler age. However, this should not be considered a positive means of identification.

Linen is not readily available today. It takes a long time to grow and prepare flax from which this cloth is made. There are many synthetic fabrics on the market, and linen is not as essential as it once was, although it is making a comeback.

The sampler shown with the Lord's Prayer worked in cross-stitch is on linen, now age darkened and a bit stained. The capital letters are in red and the remainder in black. The letter "O" in the salutation "Our Father" also has yellow and green threads. It is typical that these Bible verses should be worked into a sampler by a child of long ago. The sampler and its sentiments are still treasured today.

Turn back to Colonial times. There are historians who feel that young George Washington learned to understand his fellow countrymen better when he left his father's plantation home to become a surveyor in remote Virginia. Washington met humble frontier people who lived in one-room cabins. They were willing to share their accommodations with a stranger. Washington contrasted the way they lived and the problems they faced with his own more genteel upbringing. This helped increase his leadership ability. Perhaps in these days of machines and mass-production, it is good to own a handcrafted article from years gone by, muse over its possible story, and consider the lives of the people who owned it. This continuity of the past with the present is one of the attractions of country furniture. *Heritage, history, home united.*

# Glossary

**Apothecary chest**
Many drawers in a wooden frame used by a druggist to store pharmaceutical supplies.

**Applied**
An ornament made separately and attached to a piece.

**Apron (skirt)**
This structural aid hides construction details on tables, chairs, and case pieces. The apron or skirt is under the seat of a chair and beneath the top of a table to hide where the legs connect. It is between the feet at the base of chests, cupboards, and cabinets.

**Arrow back**
Spindles on the backs of settees or chairs that bear a resemblance to arrows.

**Bail handle**
A metal drawer pull with a half loop pendant that is fastened to a back plate.

**Balloon back**
A chair back that vaguely resembles a hot air balloon.

**Bootjack end**
A foot with a triangular cutout resembling a bootjack that holds the heel of a boot as the wearer pulls it off.

**Boston rocker**
A rocking chair with spindles in the back and a seat that curves up at the rear and under in the front. Usually painted and decorated originally.

**Breadboard ends**
Crosswise pieces of wood attached to the ends of furniture such as chest, table top or door edges to prevent warping.

**Butt joint**
The flat ends of two boards are put together with no overlap. The simplest joint. A drawer side may be attached to the front in this manner.

**Cane**
Long narrow strip of rattan (palm tree) used for weaving chair seats and backs.

**Carpet cutter (ankle skinner, cheese cutter)**
Tall rockers, higher than they are wide, and thought to damage rugs.

**Case piece**
A box like structure such as a cabinet, chest of drawers, or desk.

**Chamfer**
Bevel. A corner or edge cut off to form a slanting surface.

**Circa**
Means around or about. When accompanied by a year date, such as circa 1850, it is used to indicate an approximate year that could be two or three years before or after 1850.

**Closed cupboard**
Defined, in this book, as a cupboard with doors.

**Cobbled**
A piece with parts changed or added so that it is not in its original state. Example: a dry sink made from a cupboard.

**Comb-back Windsor**
Spindles in a comb shape that extend above the main part of the back on a Windsor chair.

**Commode**
An enclosed, cupboard-type washstand, usually including one or more drawers.

**Cornice**
The top horizontal molding on an article of furniture.

**Cottage furniture**
Inexpensive, factory produced furniture of the mid- to late-1800s that was painted with bright colored flowers, birds, or other designs. Bed-chamber furniture was often made in painted sets.

**Dough box, dough tray, dough trough**
Wooden containers in which large amounts of bread dough could be placed to rise. Those with tops served as a kneading and shaping surface for the loaves.

**Dovetail**
Joint made when the triangular projection in one board fits into a matching cut at the end of another board so they interlock as jigsaw puzzle pieces do.

**Dowel**
A peg or pin that fits into holes in two pieces of wood to hold them together. Old pegs are not perfectly round, but are slightly square in appearance.

**Drop front (fall, slant)**
A hinged lid that drops down to serve as a writing surface of a desk.

**Dry sink**
A cupboard with a well or tray, usually zinc lined, used when water was carried in, not piped into houses.

**Escutcheon**
A fitting around a keyhole that is either applied or inset. It can also refer to the back plate on bale handles.

**Fake**
A piece made and sold to fool someone or involving a misrepresentation that is fraudulent

**Fancy chair**
Almost any painted and decorated chair. While Hitchcock and other companies made them, they are usually called Hitchcock chairs.

**Fall front (drop, slant)**
A hinged lid that drops to form the writing surface of a desk.

**Finger grip**
A groove cut in the lower front edge of a drawer in place of a knob or handle.

**Finial**
A carved, cast, or turned terminal ornament on furniture; for example, pineapple finials on a bedpost.

**Flush**
Level with the surrounding surface.

**Geometric**
Designs with circles, triangles, squares, or similar outlines.

**Graining**
Artificial grain painted on wood.

**Half spindle**
Spindles that extend mid-way on the back of a chair rather than from seat to top rail. They fit into a slat.

**Hardware**
Any metal including hinges, escutcheons, nails screws, straps, and the like on a piece. Handles and pulls are considered "hardware" even when they are made of wood, glass, ivory, ceramics, or other non-metallic materials.

**Hitchcock**
From 1820-1850s, Lambert Hitchcock manufactured painted and decorated chairs similar to the English Sheraton fancy chairs. While other companies also made them, their generic (family) title is Hitchcock.

**Incised**
Design engraved or cut into the surface.

**Joiner**
An old-time craftsman did not fasten pieces together with metal. He was called a joiner because he depended on wooden pegs, dovetails, mortise and tenons, and other joints to attach parts in furniture making.

**Kerf marks**
Marks left by a saw. Usually, before the 1850s, a straight blade was used and it left up and down parallel rows called kerf marks. The circular saw makes semicircular rows and appeared in the United States about 1820, but probably was not in general use until the 1850s.

**Lap or rabbet joint**
Boards cut at a right angle so that the front of one fits into the back of another.

**Lathe**
A machine that shapes wood by holding it against a cutting tool. Turned table and chair legs are formed in this fashion.

**Marriage**
Pieces of furniture put together as one although not originally intended to be united. Example: two cupboards, a base and a top, which were separate, could be joined.

**Milk paint**
Paint with a milk base to which pigment and other ingredients are added. Homemade in the 1800s. Often red, blue, or gray.

**Miter joint**
The ends of two boards are cut at a slant and

fitted together to form a right angle. They may be pegged, nailed, or glued. Square or rectangular picture frames are frequently joined this way.

**Molding**

A continuous ornamental edging applied to or carved in furniture.

**Mortise and tenon**

A mortise is a hole or slot in a piece of wood. The tenon is a protruding prong or tongue in another piece of wood that fits tightly into the mortise to form a joint. They may be pegged to strengthen the union.

**Open cupboard**

It has no doors.

**Ogee**

A molding with a continuous double curve.

**Panel**

A rectangular or square board set in a grooved framework. A flush panel is level with the frame. A raised panel is above the surface around it, and a sunken panel is beneath the frame.

**Pegged**

A wooden pin or dowel (peg) used instead of nails or screws to hold two pieces of board together at a joint. If handmade, pegs are irregular in size and shape, appearing slightly squarish. They are not perfectly round as machined dowels are today.

**Pewter cupboard**

An open cupboard. Supposedly, pewter was displayed in it.

**Pie safe**

A closed cupboard with pierced tin panels that allowed air to circulate when pies were stored within and kept flies and rodents out. Screening and punched board panels were also used.

**Pillow rail**

An elliptical part on a top rail. Often found on Hitchcock chairs.

**Plank seat**

A seat constructed from one piece of wood.

**Projection front**

A top that protrudes out over the rest of the piece. A top drawer may stick out over the others.

**Rabbet or lap joint**

Boards where the right angle cut in the front on one slips into the right angle cut in the back of another to fit precisely.

**Reproduction (repro)**

A copy. Reproductions are fraudulent only when sold as the genuine article with an intent to deceive. Those sold as new are accepted as such.

**Rolltop**

A flexible panel made of parallel slats that slides horizontally or pulls down. Example: rolltop desk.

**Rung (stretcher, runner)**

A connecting runner or stretcher at the bottom of chair, cabinet or table leg.

**Runner**

- Rockers on chairs.
- Slides to support desk drop lids.
- Guiding strips that support drawers.
- A stretcher or rung.

**Rush**

A marsh plant from which woven chair seats can be made. Rolled paper is usually used today.

**Saddle seat**

A seat scooped out so that it fits the human body, rounded on each side and higher in the middle.

**Scalloped**

Continuous curves in a decorative edge that resemble the pattern on a shell.

**Scribe line**

Handmade articles are marked with a sharp instrument that cuts a narrow, shallow groove to show how and where two pieces of furniture should be joined.

**Settee**

A light, open seat with a low back, about double the width of a chair.

**Settle**

A wooden, high-back settee with solid sides to protect sitters from drafts.

**Shaker**

A religious community that designed, constructed, and sold high quality furniture, baskets, boxes, and other objects. Shaker chairs have simple fragile lines but are durable. Slatbacks (ladder backs) with woven seats were popular.

**Skirt (apron)**

A piece that hides construction details such as where legs join a table or chair seat, or near the base on cabinets, chests, and cupboards.

**Slant front (fall, drop)**

The hinged drop-lid on a desk that forms a writing surface when dropped down and slants back when closed.

**Slat**

Horizontal cross bar in chair backs.

**Spindle**

A slender, shaped rod, often in chair backs such as Windsors.

**Splat**

A central upright in a chair back, either plain or decorative.

**Splay**

Slant out, especially chair legs that slant out from seat to floor. Rake and cant are other terms for splay.

**Spool turning**

Appears to be spools, knobs, balls or similar items strung in a continuous row. Table legs and spindles may have spool turnings. Some beds are spool beds.

**Stretchers (rung, runner)**

Rungs or crosspieces that connect chair legs, tables, or cabinets.

**Tape**

The strips of colored fabric used by Shakers to weave chair seats.

**Tenon**

A prong or tongue that fits snugly into a mortise (hole or slot) to join two furniture parts together. May be pegged.

**Tongue and groove**

A continuous tongue sticking out at the end of one board to fit into a corresponding groove cut in another to which it is to be joined.

**Turning**

Wood shaped on a lathe to form table and chair legs or other turned pieces.

**Veneer**

A thin layer of decorative wood glued over the surface of another wood to add beauty to a piece.

**Wardrobe**

A piece of furniture in which clothes are hung.

**Wedge**

A piece of wood that tapers at the edge. May be inserted into an open tenon to make it expand to fit tighter. (A leg that goes through a seat of a chair may have a wedge added.)

**Windsor chair**

Graceful chairs with many slender, shaped spindles and splayed legs (slanting out).

**Wing**

Solid sides that project to block off drafts. Used on cradles, chairs, or settles.

# Bibliography

Aronson, Joseph. *Encyclopedia of Furniture*. New York, N.Y.: Crown Publishers Inc., 1965.

Bradford, Ernie. *Dictionary of Antiques*. London, England: The English Universities Press Ltd., 1963.

Fisher, Leonard Everett. *The Cabinetmaker*. New York, N.Y.: Franklin Watts, Inc., 1966.

Gould, Mary Earle. *Antique Tin and Tole Ware*. Rutland, Vt.: Charles E. Tuttle Co., Inc., 1949.

Gould, Mary Earle. *The Early American House*. Rutland, Vt.: Charles E. Tuttle Co., Inc., 1958.

Horst, Mel, and Smith, Elmer L. *Early Country Furniture*. Lebanon, Pa.: Applied Arts Publishers, 1970.

Ormsbee, Thomas H. *The Windsor Chair*. New York, N.Y.: Deerfield Books, Inc., distributed by Hearthside Press, Inc., 1962.

Smith, Nancy A. *Old Furniture: Understanding the Craftsman's Art*. Boston, Mass., and Toronto, Canada: Little, Brown and Company, 1975.

Winchester, Alice. *How To Know American Antiques*. New York, N.Y., and Toronto, Canada: The New American Library, 1951.

# Index

♣ ♣ ♣

# About the Authors

**B**ob and Harriett Swedberg especially enjoy collecting antiques because of the fine friendships they have made with others who share this interest. This hobby links the generations, binds various nationalities together, and spans economic barriers. The Swedbergs like to share their knowledge through teaching classes, conducting seminars, lecturing, and exhibiting items at antique shows. These Moline, Illinois, residents are members of "Speakers' Corner" (309-794-0505) and are available for programs. They have written columns and have been featured guests on many radio and television programs.